D1395802

Edinburgh

Berlitz Publishing Company, Inc.

Princeton   Mexico City   Dublin   Eschborn   Singapore

Text:	Lindsay Bennett
Editor:	Richard Wallis
Photography:	Pete Bennett except pages 5 and 88 by Neil Wilson
Cover Photo:	Pete Bennett
Photo Editor:	Naomi Zinn
Layout:	Media Content Marketing, Inc.
Cartography:	Ortelius Design

Although the publisher tries to insure the accuracy of all the information in this book, changes are inevitable and errors may result. The publisher cannot be responsible for any resulting loss, inconvenience, or injury. If you find an error in this guide, please let the editors know by writing to Berlitz Publishing Company, 400 Alexander Park, Princeton, NJ 08540-6306.

ISBN 2-8315-7695-4

Printed in Italy
010/007 REV

CONTENTS

● A  in the text denotes a highly recommended sight

Edinburgh

EDINBURGH AND
ITS PEOPLE

Every day except Sunday, at one o'clock in the afternoon, a loud boom splits the air, shattering the calm of visitors yet prompting locals merely to glance at their wristwatches. A twenty-five pound gun set on a battery of the imposing castle above the town has fired a single shell. The sound fades into the distance as the smoke from its muzzle dissipates into the clear air. This is Edinburgh, a city which, since 1846, has marked time in its own distinctive style and to which, in return, time has bequeathed a rich legacy of monuments, myths, martyrs, and memories that make it a magnet for visitors.

The city of Edinburgh is the capital of the nation of Scotland. It sits in the east of the country, 5-km (3-miles) south of the estuary of the River Forth and 605-km (378-miles) north of London, the capital of the United Kingdom. It was founded in an amazing geological area on hills created by ancient volcanic activity — ideal vantage points for building strong defenses and spying an approaching enemy.

The allure of Edinburgh is its complexity: It's like a jewel with several facets. Look at it from different angles and you will discover something new each time.

The town became the "principal burgh" of the kingdom during the reign of James III (1460–1488), and in the following years it blossomed. Complete districts from that time are still in place, replete with multi-story houses (called tenements or "lands"), churches, taverns, and tollhouses. These are crisscrossed by numerous narrow alleys called "wynds" and separated by open spaces where markets were held, royal decrees were heard, and criminals were hanged in front of large and enthusiastic crowds.

Take a stroll through these wynds today, especially at dusk when the pale glow of the streetlamps softens the shadows. It is possible to imagine the activities of the population five centuries ago: officials going about the king's business or off to the tavern, children playing noisy street games, or "fishwives" on the street corners selling shucked oysters from the town of Leith (on the coast three miles away). Fortunately, it is less easy to conjure up the smells of that time. Sewage was thrown into the streets from upstairs windows, accompanied by shouts of "Gardeyloo!" (derived from the French "Guarde de l'eau!" or "Beware of the water!"). Strolling would not have been as pleasant an experience as it is today.

> **Other Edinburgh festivals: the Science Festival, Children's Festival, and Folk Festival.**

Three hundred years later, in the 1760s, this medieval city spawned a sibling. The "New Town," which was planned by architect James Craig and embellished by Robert Adam, became one of the most beautiful Georgian cities of the world. Today it is still very much complete, rivaled only in size and grandeur by Russia's St. Petersburg. One can easily imagine ladies in crinolines and bonnets walking along the thoroughfares, with carriages riding noisily over the cobbled streets.

The spirit engendered by the creation of the New Town brought about the new "Age of Enlightenment" for Edinburgh. Although it ceased to be a political capital in 1707 (when Scotland joined with England to create the United Kingdom), Edinburgh was at the forefront of intellectual debate. The Scottish arts were in the ascendant, with novelist Sir Walter Scott creating such works as *Rob Roy* and *Ivanhoe* and poet Robert Burns composing his epic poetry.

In modern times the handsome Georgian New Town and noble medieval Old Town live happily side by side. Their very different characters offer visitors "two cities for the price of one."

Edinburgh watches over many of Scotland's national treasures with great pride. Edinburgh Castle is a treasure in itself — and with more than one million visitors each year also Scotland's most popular attraction. Its strong walls guard not only jewels and royal artifacts but also the memories of thousands of historic events. There are three national art galleries featuring the work of masters from around the world. You'll find a Royal Palace dating back to the 15th century and two Parliament buildings, one left

You won't be able to miss the bright red phone booths along the Royal Mile.

powerless in 1707 and the other newly empowered in 1999. Three major museums illustrate Edinburgh's fascinating history, with one holding a collection revealing the annals of Scotland's past and the lives of her most illustrious sons and daughters.

Yet one of the delights of the city is that it is not simply a collection of heartless historic façades. It is instead a living, thriving community. The tenements of the Old Town and Georgian buildings of the New Town are still in residential use, with a range of stores, restaurants, pubs, and theaters sustaining the population. Edinburgh is compact, a city where you can walk to appointments or to your evening entertainment. It has few tall buildings. With its proximity to the countryside — only ten minutes in any direction to the seashore or unbroken green hills — it comes as no surprise to learn that it has been confirmed as one of the most congenial places to live in the UK.

The people of Edinburgh are often accused by their fellow Scots of lacking passion and have been labeled "prim and proper." One reason for this could be that they have traditionally pursued such conservative, respectable vocations as banking, medicine, law, and academia. But this wealth of earnest achievement doesn't mean that the people lack verve or the ability to enjoy themselves. It is simply that the serious aspects of life are given their proper due before the fun can begin.

Edinburgh's people are some of the most friendly and welcoming you could hope to meet: they are quite genuine and unaffected. The city's urbane residents enjoy their galleries,

View Edinburgh the old-fashioned way — from the open top of a vintage red bus. You'll be able to see it all!

theaters, and exhibitions as much as visitors do. Their restaurants feature internationally renowned chefs who create dishes using some of the finest meat, game, and fish in the world. People here love to socialize, and they get together in hundreds of pubs, each with its own character. Old Town pubs hark back to the days of Burns and Scott, with small, smoky rooms and low lighting. In the New Town, chic wine bars welcome the banking and insurance set for after-office rendezvous.

In 1947 the opera impresario Sir Rudolf Bing undertook the task of organizing the first annual arts festival, which aimed to attract major names in the fields of music, drama, and dance. By 1987, the Edinburgh International Festival had grown into the largest annual arts event in the world, with hundreds of performances in numerous venues across the city during August and early September. Today, however, the main arts festival is only part of a veritable circus of summer activities that seem to turn the city upside down.

Regiments of soldiers in full dress regalia march precisely to the sound of pipe and drum in the Military Tattoo, and connoisseurs of the silver screen gather for an extravaganza of offerings on celluloid. The Festival Fringe, perhaps Dr. Jekyll to the International Festival's Mr. Hyde, is an umbrella title given

Auld Reekie

In old Edinburgh almost every room in every dwelling was kept warm with an open fire, and thousands of sooty plumes rose daily above the city. Following the Industrial Revolution, factories and smoke-belching trains added to the problem. Edinburgh was given the nickname "Auld Reekie," or "Old Smoky." But after World War II the city introduced a clean-air policy and removed the sooty residue from stone buildings in the New Town, consigning Edinburgh's dark and dirty reputation to the past.

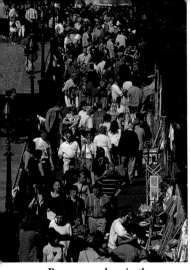

Browse or shop in the many artisans' stalls that line busy walking streets.

to thousands of performances ranging from the avant-garde to the downright irreverent. And each year at festival time, Edinburgh willingly gives its streets over to stilt walkers, automatons, satirists, and barbershop quartets along with 500,000 visitors — belying its reputation for being sober and staid.

Another wonderful time to visit Edinburgh is at the turn of the year, when the city hosts the "biggest New Year's Eve party in the world," called Hogmanay. The whole population comes out into the streets to watch a huge display of fireworks illuminate the historic skyline. Where better to sing your year-end rendition of "Auld Lang Syne"?

At the start of the new millennium, Edinburgh is once again wielding true political power on behalf of its fellow countrymen: The "Scotland Act," passed in November 1998, transferred control of domestic policy from London back to the Scots for the first time since 1707. The sense of an impending new era can be discerned in the pride, confidence, and energy of people on the city streets. It is also taking concrete form in the new Scottish Parliament building at the bottom of the Royal Mile. Edinburgh is a city with firm foundations in the past, but it also has designs on the future.

A BRIEF HISTORY

The city of Edinburgh grew up around the steep, ragged cliff of the Castle Rock and its easily defended summit. Archaeological excavations have revealed evidence of habitation here as long ago as 900 B.C. Very little, however, is known about the Rock and its inhabitants in the centuries between its first occupation and the time of the MacAlpin kings. A few shadowy details have been left to us by the Romans and by an epic poem from the seventh century.

Romans and Britons

The Romans invaded Scotland in A.D. 78–84, where they met a fierce group called the Picts, whom they drove north. They consolidated their gains by building Antonine's Wall across the waist of Scotland between the Firth of Forth and the River Clyde in about A.D. 150.

Roman legions encountered the strongholds of the Castle Rock and Arthur's Seat, held by a tribe of ancient Britons known as the Votadini. Little is recorded about this group, but they were probably the ancestors of the Gododdin, whose feats are told in a seventh-century Old Welsh manuscript. The capital of the Gododdin was Din Eidyn (the "Fort of Eidyn," almost certainly the Castle Rock), whose name lives on in the *Edin-* of *Edinburgh*. Din Eidyn fell to the Angles in 638 and became part of the Anglian kingdom of Northumbria. It was the first of many times that the Fort of Eidyn would change hands between the kingdoms of the north and the south.

The MacAlpin Kings

Four distinct peoples once inhabited the land now known as Scotland: the Picts in the north, the Britons in the southwest, the invading Angles in the southeast, and the Scots in the west. The

Scots were Gaelic-speaking immigrants from the north of Ireland. Kenneth MacAlpin, who ruled as king of Scots at Dunadd, acquired the Pictish throne in 843, uniting Scotland north of the River Forth into a single kingdom. He moved his capital — along with the Stone of Destiny (on which Scottish kings were crowned) — to the sacred Pict site of Scone, close to Perth. His great-great-great-grandson, Malcolm II (1005–1034), defeated the Angles at the Battle of Carham in 1018 and extended Scottish territory as far south as the River Tweed. These new lands included the stronghold of Edinburgh.

Malcolm II's own grandson, Malcolm Canmore (1058–1093), often visited Edinburgh with his wife Margaret, a Saxon princess. They crossed the Forth from Dunfermline at the narrows known to this day as Queensferry. Margaret was a deeply pious woman who was subsequently canonized, and her youngest son, David I (1124–1153), founded a church in her name on the highest point of the Castle Rock (St. Margaret's Chapel). David also founded the Abbey of Holyrood and created several royal burghs (towns with special trading privileges), including Edinburgh and Canongate; the latter was under the jurisdiction of the monks, or "canons," of Holyrood.

At this time Edinburgh was still a very modest town, but David's successor, Malcolm IV (1153–1165), made its castle his main residence. By the end of the 12th century, Edinburgh's castle was used as a royal treasury. The town's High Street stretched beneath the castle along the ridge to the east (today the Royal Mile), past the parish church of St. Giles, and out to the Netherbow, where Edinburgh ended and Canongate began.

Wars of Independence

In 1286 the MacAlpin dynasty ended, leaving Scotland without a ruler. There were a number of claimants to the throne, among them John Balliol, Lord of Galloway, and Robert de Brus, Lord of Annandale. The guardians of Scotland were unable to decide who should succeed and asked the English king, Edward I, to adjudicate. Edward, seeing this invitation as a chance to assert his claim as overlord of Scotland, chose John Balliol, whom he judged to be the weaker of the two.

Edward treated King John as a vassal. However, when Edward went to war with France in 1294 and summoned John along with other knights, the Scottish king decided he had had enough. He ignored Edward's summons and instead negotiated a treaty with the French king, the beginning of a long association between France and Scotland that became known as the "Auld Alliance."

Edward was furious, and his reprisal was swift and bloody. In 1296 he led a force of nearly 30,000 men into Scotland and captured the castles of Roxburgh, Edinburgh, and Stirling. The Stone of Destiny and the Scottish crown jewels were stolen, and Scotland's Great Seal was broken up. Oaths of fealty were demanded from Scottish nobles, while English officials were installed to oversee the running of the country. Scotland became little more than an English county.

But the Scots did not take this insult lying down. Bands of rebels (such as those led by William Wallace) began to at-

The mighty "Mons Meg" — a gift to James IV from the Duke of Burgundy in 1457.

tack the English garrisons and make raids into English territory. When Wallace was captured, the Scots looked for a new leader and discovered one in Robert the Bruce, grandson of the Robert de Brus rejected by Edward in 1292. He was crowned King of Scots at Scone in 1306 and began his campaign to drive the English out of Scotland.

Edward I died in 1307 and was succeeded by his ineffectual son, Edward II, who in 1314 led an army of some 25,000 men to confront Bruce's army at Bannockburn, near Stirling. Though outnumbered, the Scots gained a famous victory and sent the English packing. Robert the Bruce continued to harass the English until they were forced to sue for peace. A truce was declared, and the Treaty of Northampton was negotiated at Edinburgh in 1328.

Two of the recurring themes of Scottish history are minors inheriting the throne and divided loyalties. Although many Scottish nobles were dedicated to the cause of independence, others either bore grudges against the ruling king or held lands in England that they feared to lose. These divisions — later hardened by religious schism — would forever deny Scotland a truly united voice.

When Robert the Bruce died in 1329, his son and heir, David II, was only five years old. Within a few years the wars with England resumed, aggravated by civil war at home as Edward Balliol (son of John) tried to take the Scottish throne with the help of the English king, Edward III.

The Stewart Dynasty

During these stormy years, the castle of Edinburgh was occupied several times by English garrisons. In 1341 it was taken from the English by William of Douglas. The young David II returned from exile in France and made it his principal royal residence, building a tower house (David's Tower) on the site of what is now the Half Moon Battery. He died in 1371 and was succeeded by his nephew, Robert II. David's sister Marjory had married Walter the Steward, and their son was the first of the long line of Stewart (later spelled *Stuart)* monarchs who would reign over Scotland — and, subsequently, Great Britain — until the "Glorious Revolution" of 1688.

The strength and wealth of Scotland increased during the reigns of the first Stewart kings. New castles were built and new weapons acquired, including the famous gun called "Mons Meg." Edinburgh emerged as Scotland's main political center and was declared by James III (1460–1488) to be "the principal burgh of our kingdom."

James IV (1488–1513) confirmed Edinburgh's status as the capital of Scotland by constructing a royal palace at Holyrood. He cemented a peace treaty with England by marrying Margaret Tudor, the daughter of Henry VII — the so-called Marriage of the Thistle and the Rose — but this did not prevent him from making a raid into England in 1513. The attack culminated in the disastrous Battle of Flodden, near the River Tweed, and the king was killed. Fearing invasion, the Edinburgh town council built a protective wall (the "Flodden Wall") around the city boundaries.

Yet again a minor — the infant James V — succeeded to the throne, and Scots nobles were divided as to whether Scotland should draw closer to England or seek help from her old ally, France. The adult James leaned toward France and in 1537 took a French wife, Mary of Guise. She bore two sons who both died in infancy, but by the time she was about to give birth to their third child, her husband lay dying at Falkland Palace. On 8 December 1542 a messenger arrived with news that the queen had produced a daughter at the palace of Linlithgow. A few days later the king was dead, leaving a week-old baby girl to inherit the Scottish crown.

Mary, Queen of Scots

The baby was Mary Stuart, who at the age of nine months was crowned Queen of Scots at the Chapel Royal, Stirling. When the news reached London, Henry VIII saw his chance to subdue Scotland again and negotiated a marriage between the infant Mary and his son Edward. The Scots refused, and Henry sent an army rampaging through Scotland on a campaign known as the "Rough Wooing." The English king ordered his general to "burn Edinburgh town so there may remain forever a perpetual memory of the vengeance of God lightened upon the Scots."

But more was at stake than simply Scotland's independence: there was now a religious schism within Britain. In order to divorce Catherine of Aragon and marry Anne Boleyn, Henry

The "Honours of Scotland" exhibition includes this life-like King James IV display, replete with fine jewels.

VIII had broken with Rome and brought the English church under his own control. England was thus now a Protestant country, caught between Catholic France and the Scots with their new Catholic queen.

The Scots themselves were divided, many embracing Protestantism in the spirit of the Reformation while others remained staunchly Catholic. However, fear of the rampaging English army led the Scots again to seek help from their old allies in France, and the young queen married the Dauphin François, son of the French king.

François II became king of France in 1559 but died soon after. In 1561 the 18-year-old Mary returned to a Scotland in the grip of the Reformation, as Protestant leaders had taken control of the Scottish parliament and abolished the authority of the pope. Her Protestant cousin, Elizabeth Tudor, was on the English throne, but Elizabeth — the "Virgin Queen" — had no heir. Mary was next in line for the English crown, and Elizabeth was suspicious of her intentions.

The six years of Mary's reign were turbulent ones. She clashed early on with Edinburgh's famous Protestant reformer, John Knox, who held sway in St. Giles but later adopted an uneasy policy of religious tolerance. In 1565 she married her young cousin Henry, Lord Darnley, much to the chagrin of Elizabeth (Darnley was a grandson of Margaret Tudor and thus also had a claim to the English throne). On 19 June 1566, in the royal apartments in Edinburgh Castle, Mary gave birth to a son, Prince James.

Within a year, however, Darnley was murdered, and Mary immediately immersed herself in controversy by marrying the Earl of Bothwell, the chief suspect. Mary was forced to abdicate in 1567, and the infant prince was crowned as James VI.

Mary sought asylum in England, only to be imprisoned by Elizabeth. The English queen kept her cousin in captivity for

20 years and finally had her beheaded on a trumped-up charge of treason. So it was bitterly ironic when Elizabeth died without an heir and James, Mary's Catholic son, inherited the English throne.

In 1603 James VI of Scotland was thus crowned James I of England, marking the Union of the Crowns. Although Scotland was still a separate kingdom, the two countries would from that day be ruled by the same monarch.

The Covenanters

Edinburgh's population grew fast between 1500 and 1650, and a maze of tall, unsanitary tenements sprouted along the spine of the High Street. The castle was extended, and in 1582 the Town's College (the precursor of the University of Edinburgh) was founded. James died in 1625, succeeded by his son, Charles I, who proved an incompetent ruler. In 1637 his attempt to force the Scottish Presbyterian Church to accept an English liturgy and the rule of bishops led to civil revolt and rioting.

The next year, a large group of Scottish churchmen and nobles signed the National Covenant, a declaration condemning the new liturgy and pledging allegiance to the Presbyterian faith. The Covenanters, as they were called, at first sided with Oliver Cromwell's Parliamentarians in the civil war that had erupted across the border. But when the English revolutionaries beheaded Charles I in 1649, the Scots rallied round his son, Charles II. Cromwell's forces then invaded Scotland, crushed the Covenanter army, and went on to take Edinburgh. Scotland suffered ten years of military rule under Cromwell's Commonwealth.

Scotland's troubles continued after Charles II's restoration to the throne in 1660. The Covenanters faced severe persecution at the hands of the king's supporters, who had decided to follow his father's policy of imposing bishops on the Scots. Hundreds of Covenanters were imprisoned and executed.

In the end England underwent the "Glorious Revolution" of 1688, when Catholic James II (Scotland's James VII) was deposed and the Protestant William of Orange (1689–1702) took the British crown. Presbyterianism was established as Scotland's official state church and the Covenanters prevailed.

Act of Union

On 1 May 1707 England and Scotland were formally joined together by the "Act of Union" — establishing the Union of Parliaments — and the United Kingdom was born. Despite the fact that Scotland was allowed to retain its own legal system, education system, and national Presbyterian Church, the move was opposed by the great majority of Scots. The supporters of the deposed James VII and his successors, exiled in France, were known as the "Jacobites." Several times during the next 40 years they attempted to restore the Stuart dynasty to the British throne, though by this time the crown had passed to the German House of Hanover.

James Edward Stuart, known as the "Old Pretender," traveled up the Firth of Forth in 1708 but was driven back by British ships and bad weather. Another campaign was held in 1715 under the Jacobite Earl of Mar, but it was the 1745 rising of Prince Charles Edward Stuart, the "Young Pretender," which became the stuff of legend.

The prince, known as Bonnie Prince Charlie (the grandson of James VII), raised an army of Jacobite highlanders and swept through Scotland. They occupied Edinburgh (but not the castle) and defeated a government army at the Battle of Prestonpans. In November of that year he invaded England, capturing Carlisle and driving south as far as Derby, only 200 km (130 miles) short of London.

Finding his forces outnumbered and overextended here, the young prince beat a tactical retreat, but the English army hounded him relentlessly. The final showdown — at Culloden in 1746 — saw the Jacobite army slaughtered. Prince Charlie fled and was pursued over the Highlands before escaping in a French ship. He died in Rome in 1788, disillusioned and drunk.

The Scottish Enlightenment

The Jacobite uprisings found little support in such lowland cities as Edinburgh. Here there was a growing sense that the Union was around to stay. Within ten years of the Young Pretender's occupation of Holyrood, Edinburgh's town council proposed a plan to relieve the chronic overcrowding of the Royal Mile tenements by constructing a New Town on land to the north of the castle. In 1767 a design by a young and previously unknown architect, James Craig, was approved and work began.

This architectural renaissance in Edinburgh was followed by an intellectual flowering in the sciences, philosophy, and medicine that revolutionized Western society in the late 18th century and saw the city dubbed the "Athens of the North." Famous Edinburgh residents of this period — later known as the Scottish Enlightenment — included David Hume, author of *A Treatise of Human Nature* and one of Britain's greatest philosophers; Adam Smith, author of *The Wealth of Nations,* a pioneer in the study of political economy; and Joseph Black, the scientist who discovered the concept of latent heat. Robert Burns's poems and Walter Scott's novels rekindled interest in Scotland's history and nationhood; Scott especially worked hard to raise Scotland's profile.

The Modern City

In the 19th century Edinburgh was swept up in the Industrial Revolution. The coalfields of Lothian and Fife fueled the growth of baking, distilling, printing, and machine-making industries, giving Edinburgh the epithet "Auld Reekie" (Old Smoky). With the arrival of the railways in the mid-1800s, the city grew almost exponentially as new lines led to the spread of Victorian suburbs such as Marchmont and Morningside.

During the 20th century Edinburgh became a European center of learning and culture. The University of Edinburgh has made outstanding contributions to various fields. The Edinburgh International Festival (held annually since 1947) is acknowledged as one of the world's most important arts festivals. In addition, the city's rich history and architecture have made it one of the most popular tourist destinations in the United Kingdom.

Nationalism never completely disappeared, however, and in the latter part of the century there has been a concerted (though peaceful) effort to gain self-determination for Scotland. In 1979 the nationalists were in disarray when a referendum was defeated, and further efforts came to nought during Conservative rule in the British Parliament at Westminster through the 1980s and early 1990s. But the Stone of Destiny was returned to Scottish soil in 1996 — 700 years after it had been taken south by the English.

The criss-crossed tracks leaving the Waverly railway station make perfect sense!

The general election of May 1997 proved to be a turning point. The British Labour Party supported the return of domestic policy-making power to Scotland. When it was victorious at the ballot box, among the new government's first tasks was to organize a referendum on Scottish devolution. This took place in September 1997, with the majority supporting the creation of a Scottish Parliament, although many strident nationalists thought the proposals did not go far enough. The Scotland Bill was put before the British Parliament in January 1998 and became law as the "Scotland Act" in November 1998.

Political power thus returned to Edinburgh after nearly 300 years. Elections were held in May 1999, and the new Parliament opened on the first of July. The city now buzzes with energy and confidence as MPs and policy makers gather to make plans for the future of the Scottish people.

The Duke of Wellington sits atop his trusty steed on Princes Street, steps from the National Gallery of Scotland.

Historical Landmarks

900 B.C. late-Bronze/early-Iron Age settlement on Castle Rock.

first–second centuries A.D. Roman occupation of southern Scotland; hill fort of the Votadini tribe on Castle Rock.

843 Scotland north of the Forth united under Kenneth MacAlpin.

1124–1157 reign of David I, founder of Abbey of Holyrood.

1297 Scots rebels under Wallace defeat English at Stirling Bridge.

1314 Scots victory under Robert the Bruce at Bannockburn.

1513 Scots suffer defeat at Flodden; Edinburgh builds city walls.

1544 the Rough Wooing: Henry VIII's forces sack Edinburgh.

1559–1572 John Knox is minister of St. Giles.

1560 Protestantism is established as Scotland's national faith.

1561–1567 Mary, Queen of Scots, lives in Holyrood Palace.

1571–1573 the "Lang Siege" badly damages Edinburgh Castle.

1603 Union of the Crowns: James VI of Scotland becomes James I of England.

1638 the National Covenant is signed at Greyfriars Kirkyard.

1689 William of Orange invited to take over government of Scotland; civil war between William and Jacobites.

1707 "Act of Union" and creation of the United Kingdom; Scottish Parliament dissolved.

1745 Jacobite uprising; Bonnie Prince Charlie's army occupies Holyrood.

1767 construction of Edinburgh's New Town begins.

1844 Sir Walter Scott Monument is completed.

1890 Forth Railway Bridge opens.

1947 the first Edinburgh International Festival.

1979 referendum on creation of a Scottish assembly is defeated.

1996 Stone of Destiny returned to Scotland.

1997 Labour Party wins British general election.

1998 referendum on Scottish devolution receives a majority vote; the "Scotland Act" becomes law.

1999 Scottish elections held; first "new" Parliament opens 1 July.

WHERE TO GO

A city of several different ages, Edinburgh has distinct districts that are all eminently walkable. You can divide your visit into three or four separate tours, each of which could fill either an afternoon or an entire day. There are also bus tours around the city to help you get your bearings before you visit special attractions. The buses stand in line on Waverley Street near the main railway station.

THE OLD TOWN

Edinburgh's **Old Town** occupies an amazing site where the geology has its own fascinating story to tell. The Castle Rock and Arthur's Seat are the remains of lava streams that hardened after the two volcanoes around them became dormant and cold. During the last Ice Age, huge glaciers covered the region, moving west to east across the land and gouging trenches on either side of the volcanic mounds. They resisted the great power of the ice and caused a long stream of sediment to collect. At the end of the Ice Age (some 13,000 years ago), the glaciers melted, leaving a long ridge of sediment sloping gradually from the top of the volcanic hills.

When the castle was built atop the hill, the original city of Edinburgh grew on this ridge, reaching down in a ribbon of development toward the Abbey of Holyrood, at the foot of the hill in the east. In the 16th century, a strong city wall — now almost completely destroyed — protected the population. Combined with the geological setting of the city, this stifled development. Instead of expanding outward, the city had no choice but to grow upward.

The famous tenements (or "lands") began to be built. At least 6 stories high, they were reached through narrow alleys called "closes" or "wynds" that became the focus of city life.

A constant cycle of building, decay, collapse, and rebuilding — plus the occasional catastrophic fire — gave the Old Town its characteristic irregular layout and chimney-strewn skyline.

Edinburgh Castle

The castle has always been considered the heart of Edinburgh, but its site is older than the city itself: Excavations show evidence of settlement in the Bronze Age (ca. 900 B.C.). It dominates the skyline, sitting atop Castle Rock. The dramatically rising cliff of black basalt stone made the castle impregnable to all but the most wily commander. It was the seat of power for anyone who ruled the region, control of which passed from Scotland to England many times over the centuries.

Following the "Act of Union" with England in 1707, the castle lost its strategic importance but later, in Victorian times, experienced a rebirth. The Victorians reworked the his-

As the sky darkens, Edinburgh Castle is aglow, dominating the skyline with its formidable walls and towering turrets.

Monday to Saturday at 1pm sharp, the One O'Clock Gun is fired, causing unprepared tourists to jump at the blast.

tory and legends of Scotland to add romantic, neo-Gothic touches. They also greatly expanded the castle, for decorative purposes rather than for defense. Today Edinburgh Castle is the most-visited attraction in Scotland, with more than one million people passing through the entrance gate each year.

A visit to the castle will take at least two hours, but many people spend far longer there. There is an informative recorded tape in several languages (you listen on headphones as you tour the attractions) to help you make the most of your visit. The extremely helpful and knowledgeable staff is more than happy to answer any questions that you have.

Your first view of the castle will be the **Gate House,** which you pass through to reach the inner "wards." Built between 1886 and 1888, the Gate House was a Victorian attempt to recapture the medieval castle style, but it was more a cosmetic addition than a defensive structure. The dry ditches in front, however, date from the 1650s. In the 1920s bronze statues of two Scottish heroes — William Wallace and Robert the Bruce — were added to the façade. In summer you will find an honor guard of kilted soldiers standing sentry on the walkway over the ditches.

Once inside, you will find yourself in the lower ward, the area of the castle that has been most heavily bombarded in many military campaigns. The Old Guard House now houses one of four gift shops in the castle grounds. The walkway here once had a ditch and drawbridge to protect the inner gate, called **Portcullis Gate,** which was reconstructed in the late 16th century on 14th-century foundations. It was the main entrance to the castle, and a formidable obstacle to the enemy.

Passing through Portcullis Gate, you enter the middle ward of the castle. To your right is the **Argyll Battery,** with a line of muzzle-loading eighteen-pound guns pointing out over the skyline of the New Town (a prime spot for spectacular photography shots). To your right are the "Lang Stairs," which lead up to the medieval castle. Walk along past the battery to the Cart Shed, built in the aftermath of the Jacobian uprising in 1746. It now houses the castle café — with a good selection of snacks and hot meals — but was originally used to store the provisions carts. Beside the café is Mills Mount Battery, the location of the **One O'Clock Gun,** fired daily except Sunday at — you guessed it — 1pm. Be prepared, for it is indeed noisy.

The cobbled street leads inexorably upward, past the Governor's House and the New Barracks, neither of which is open to visitors. Eventually you will reach Foog's Gate, but take a right before you travel through the gate and follow the path around to the **Castle Vaults.** These were cut into the

Castle Rock in the 15th century to create an extra floor of space; they offer a fascinating insight into the lives of the ordinary soldiers in days gone by. The vaults were used for a variety of mundane activities (bakery and storehouse) but also functioned as a prison and barracks. Prisoners, soldiers, and the soldiers' families endured the same harsh conditions. You'll see messages on the walls of the vaults carved by French prisoners during their captivity.

In the very bowels of the building is one of the most famous attractions in the castle. **Mons Meg,** a gun weighing 6040 kg (6.6 tons), was a gift to James II in 1457 from his wife's uncle, Philip the Good, Duke of Burgundy. Manufactured in Mons (now in Belgium), the gun was state-of-the-art for the times, firing cannonballs weighing up to 150-kg (331-lbs).

> A cemetery in the castle grounds is the burial spot for soldiers' pets, honored and maintained for centuries.

It was a formidable weapon but weighed so much that it could be transported only 5-kms (3-miles) per day; often the fighting had finished before it could be brought into play. It was fired to celebrate the first wedding of Mary, Queen of Scots, to François II in 1558. In 1681, when fired as a birthday salute in honor of the Duke of Albany, Mons Meg burst her barrel and was retired from active duty.

Return to **Foog's Gate** — the name and age of the gate remain a source of debate — to enter the upper ward and the oldest parts of the castle. Directly ahead is tiny **St. Margaret's Chapel,** said to have been built by David I in the early 12th century in honor of his mother, Queen Margaret, who died in 1093. It is the oldest building in Edinburgh and is still the site of weddings and baptisms. Although the chapel has been renovated since its construction, you will find a wonderful example of a Romanesque arch in the interior. The stained-glass windows, one featuring a likeness of Margaret, were inserted into the existing openings in the 1920s.

Another set of batteries can be found in an open area south of the chapel. They are built on the site of **David's Tower,** once the largest and most formidable structure in the castle. Begun in 1368, it was the main royal lodging for centuries until it was battered and left a wreck during the "Lang Siege" of 1571–73. The remains of the tower — the rooms in its foundations — are currently being restored.

Crown Square

At the very pinnacle of the upper ward is **Crown Square,** a beautiful collection of buildings housing the treasures of Scotland. On your right as you enter the square is the **Scottish National War Memorial,** the highest building in the city. The building was originally a barracks building but was suitably refurbished by Sir Robert Lorimer in 1923 to commemorate the Scots who fell in World War I; the halls of remembrance now also commemorate those who died in World War II and all other conflicts. Inside are leather-bound regimental books with each serviceperson's name duly inscribed. Splendidly ornate stone

St. Margaret's Chapel is the oldest standing building in Edinburgh today.

View historic weapons in the Great Hall of Edinburgh Castle.

friezes realistically depict battle scenes of World War I, with each branch of the forces represented. There is also a chapel dedicated to women who sacrificed their lives for their country.

Opposite the memorial is the **Great Hall,** built in 1503 for the wedding reception of James IV and the English Mary Tudor. It was later used as the ceremonial and legislative chamber. The original "hammer-beam" wooden roof is the highlight of the design, with thick beams and painted decorations. Be sure to see the monogram of James — *IR4* — on some of the stone brackets, along with the red rose and the thistle signifying the new alliance of Scotland and England. The hall was used as a barracks through much of its later history before being renovated in 1887. The interior décor now says much more about the Victorians' romantic image of Scotland than it does about how the room would have really looked: The walls are lined with suits of armor and swords.

Along the east side of Crown Square is the **Royal Palace,** home to the most precious of the country's treasures: the Royal Regalia of Scotland. The palace, much altered over the generations, was generally used as a residence only at times of dynastic importance or danger, when Holyrood, down in the lowland, was difficult to defend. On 19 June

1566 Mary Stuart gave birth to her son James (the future James VI of Scotland and James I of England) in the small antechamber off a larger room known as **Queen Mary's Room.** The last monarch to spend a night in the palace was Charles I, in 1633.

On the upper floors (once the royal chambers) there is an exhibition telling the story of the royal regalia. Called the **Honours of Scotland,** these are said to be the oldest complete set — crown, scepter, and sword — in Europe, unchanged since 1640. There are displays of artisans creating the jewels — look for models with an uncanny resemblance to John Lennon and Paul McCartney. The highlights of the tour are "the honours" themselves, lying on blue velvet in a secure glass cabinet in the Crown Room. The Scottish crown was fashioned of gold mined in Scotland, greatly embellished during the reign of Scotland's James III (1460–1488). The scepter and sword were each papal gifts, the former in 1494 and the latter in 1507; these reinforced the links between Scotland and

---

French Prisoners and the King's Money

The Seven Year War against the French, begun in 1757, saw the vaults beneath the Great Hall turned into a camp for prisoners of war. By the end of hostilities there were over 500 French soldiers held here. They were not kept in close confinement, however, and spent their time working on handicrafts such as carved bone combs, which they sold at the Friday market. The money they earned subsidized their meager rations, but a few prisoners went further: they fashioned bone dies from which they printed forged banknotes. The notes were so expert that, for a time, they passed in the city as the genuine article.

Rome. Following union with England in 1707, however, there was little use for the Scottish regalia. They were locked in a trunk in a sealed room in Edinburgh Castle for 111 years before Sir Walter Scott received permission to open the room in 1818.

Next to the regalia sits the **Stone of Destiny,** or Stone of Scone, which historically served as the seat on which Scottish kings were crowned, a symbol of the land over which they would rule. In 1296 the stone was captured by the English from its resting place in Scone Abbey and taken to London. It has been used during crowning ceremonies for all English (then British) monarchs since that time, sitting under the coronation throne throughout the ceremony. In 1996 the stone was returned to Scotland amid great pomp, though it will make the journey to Westminster Abbey in London when the next coronation of a British monarch takes place.

On the lower floor of the Royal Palace, **Laich Hall** has been restored as closely as possible to its 1617 décor, using traditional techniques and colors. This was where the monarch met advisers and diplomats.

Leaving the castle, you will walk across the **Esplanade,** a broad open area originally created for regimental drill practice. Today it is usually used as the castle parking lot, but it offers superb views of both Princes Street to the north and the Old Town to the south. In August each year, the Esplanade is filled by a temporary arena erected for performances of the Military Tattoo.

 ## The Royal Mile

The town of Edinburgh eventually spread out below the castle, with a main street leading out the entrance and down to Holyrood Palace. In the 16th century this thoroughfare

Edinburgh Highlights

Charlotte Square: some of the finest examples of Georgian architecture in Britain surround this green area.

Edinburgh Castle: historic castle stronghold set dramatically on volcanic rocks. The Scottish crown jewels and Stone of Destiny are on display here.

Edinburgh International Festival: the world's largest and liveliest arts gathering, featuring the foremost names in music, opera, dance, and theater.

Edinburgh Military Tattoo: colorful displays featuring regimental marching, horsemanship, mock battles, dancers, and massed pipe-and-drum bands.

Museum of Scotland and **Royal Museum**: the former tells the story of the history of Scotland in a dramatic building opened in the late 1990s; the latter is housed in the adjoining Victorian edifice with collections devoted to scientific, ethnographic, archaeological, and fine-art pursuits.

Our Dynamic Earth: an interactive museum telling the story of the creation and development of the planet.

Palace of Holyroodhouse: royal palace since the 16th century and official residence of the British monarch in Scotland.

Royal Yacht Britannia: the vessel that transported the British royal family on diplomatic visits and vacations around the globe.

St. Giles Cathedral: High Kirk of Edinburgh, scene of John Knox's Protestant sermons.

Calton Hill: Offers spectacular views of the city and its skyline.

Hogmanay: A week of processions and performances in the week before New Year.

became known as the **Royal Mile** because it was the route used by royalty to make their way from the castle to Holyrood. Although a mile long, its name is misleading because it is not one street but several different streets. In former times it even crossed the old outer boundary of Edinburgh before it reached the palace.

Since the route has never seen any major redevelopment, it has grown haphazardly but organically over the centuries. Some of the buildings date from the 16th century, but it is also lined with buildings of almost every era, including numerous 17th- and 18th-century tenements called "lands," sometimes 13 stories high. These were the residential areas of the city, considered desirable when they were first built. Later they were often home to many large families, rife with over-crowding and unsanitary conditions. A stroll along the Royal Mile will take around 30-minutes, but stop and explore the various attractions on its path and you might find that this one-mile journey will last a whole day.

Before you leave the castle's Esplanade, be sure to see the small bronze fountain on the wall to the left of the entrance. This is the **Witches Well,** marking

Camera obscuras like the one atop Castlehill were all the rage in the 19th century.

the spot where women condemned for black magic were burned at the stake.

Beyond the Esplanade you enter the first section of the Royal Mile, a narrow, cobbled street called **Castlehill.** On your left you will find the **Edinburgh Old Town Weaving Company,** where you can follow the journey of wool from the sheep to the finished product. You can watch a tartan pattern

> If you visit the camera obscura at noon, there will be fewer shadows to obstruct the images.

being woven by machine and then choose from over 150 tartans in the shop. There is an exhibition of highland dress, showing how it developed through the centuries. There are also gift shops selling quality Scottish products. The building itself was at one time the major water storage facility for the wealthy residents of the New Town. Built in 1850, it had a capacity of 1.5 million-gallons of water.

Next to the weaving center, across narrow Ramsey Street, are the **Outlook Tower** and its **camera obscura,** set high above the tenement chimneystacks. A series of lenses and prisms projects a live image of the city onto a concave viewing screen inside the camera. It was built in the 1850s, when cameras were the height of fashion. Several people at one time can sit inside and watch the city at work. The experience is best when the weather is bright. There is a viewing platform around the camera, allowing first-hand viewing of the cityscape; there are also helpful explanatory maps pointing out the highlights on the horizon.

Across Castlehill is the **Scottish Whisky Heritage Centre,** which tells the story of the development of Scottish whisky with interesting displays. You can also explore the various tastes of this complex drink, comparing over 100 single malts. Bottles of your favorites are available in the gift shop on the first floor.

At the bottom of Castlehill, where the road meets Johnston Terrace, is the old Tolbooth Kirk (*kirk* means "church"), which has the highest steeple in the city at 73 m (239 ft). In the late 1990s the church underwent a massive renovation and now acts as the permanent center and offices for the Edinburgh International Festival. It has been re-christened the **Hub.**

Lawnmarket

Beyond the Hub, the Royal Mile is known as **Lawnmarket.** This was once the commercial center of the Old Town, including a weekly fabric market. There are several old lands found down the narrow wynds leading off the main street.

Good or Bad?

When Robert Louis Stevenson wrote *The Strange Case of Dr. Jekyll and Mr. Hyde* in 1886, it shocked genteel society. Little did people realize he had based his story on the real-life case of a local Edinburgh man.

Deacon William Brodie was a respectable cabinetmaker and locksmith who, when he closed his shop in the evening, lived another life. After dark he frequented the less respectable parts of town — gambling, cockfighting, and fathering five illegitimate children. He funded this lifestyle by stealing from his respectable customers, taking copies of the keys of cabinets and strongboxes sold in his shop and creeping into their houses to relieve them of their valuables.

Deacon Brodie was caught in the act in 1788 and was hung in front of a huge crowd. Ironically, he himself had designed improvements to the very gallows used for his execution.

Stevenson took this basic story and transformed it into a fascinating examination of human psychology.

Gladstone's Land, built in 1620, still has its period shopfronts at the roadside.

Behind Gladstone's Land is Lady Stair's Close, which leads to Lady Stair's House, now home to the **Writers' Museum.** The house (dating from 1622) has been beautifully renovated, and contains artifacts from the life of three important Scottish authors: Robert Burns, Sir Walter Scott, and Robert Louis Stevenson. You will find portraits, manuscripts, and personal effects from all three. The Stevenson exhibition on the lower floor is particularly interesting, with

This scribe is always at work — adorning the sign for the Writer's Museum.

photographs of the author traveling around the world before his untimely death at the age of 44 in Samoa.

Next to the Writers' Museum is **James Court,** built in the 1720s. The philosopher David Hume lived here and was regularly visited by the economist Adam Smith and by Dr. Samuel Johnson. The court must have been a hotbed of social reform at the time. At the corner of Lawnmarket and Bank Street is **Deacon Brodie's Tavern.** Named after the city gentleman and infamous burglar, it is one of the best-known pubs in the city. Look left down Bank Street to see the ornate façade of the Bank of Scotland headquarters, a symbol of the city's continuing important position in the financial world.

High Street

As you approach St. Giles Cathedral, the Royal Mile becomes **High Street.** On the left you will find a bronze statue of David Hume, depicted in calm, thoughtful pose.

☞   **St. Giles Cathedral,** on your right, was the original parish church for the city and has been at the center of many of its most important developments. There has been a Christian place of worship on the site since the 9th century. Parts of the interior date back to 1100 and its crown spire is 500 years old; much of the exterior, however, is from the early 19th century.

St. Giles was a cathedral for only five years of its long history. A more accurate title for the edifice is the High Kirk of Edinburgh. Yet it's not only the building itself that is fascinating; it is also its place in Scottish history. St. Giles was the church of John Knox, the great Protestant reformer. From 1559 to 1572 his fiery Calvinist sermons influenced worshippers far beyond the cathedral walls and fueled the religious discontent that split the population.

Visit the small chapel dedicated to the Most Ancient and Most Noble Order of the Thistle, the highest order of chivalry in Scotland. The order was founded by James VII (James II of England) and continues today. There are a maximum of 16 knights at any one time, headed by the reigning monarch.

Outside the cathedral you will find a statue of John Knox with Bible in hand. It was erected in 1906 not far from the reformer's supposed burial site. Nearby is a statue of Charles II on a steed. Completed in 1688, it is the oldest equestrian statue made of lead in Britain. Look also for the heart-shaped stone mosaic on the pavement here, marking the site of the Edinburgh Tolbooth. The building collected city taxes during the 14th century but fulfilled several additional functions in later centuries. It was the prison and place of execution immortalized in the novel *Heart of Midlothian,* by Sir Walter Scott. It was demolished in 1817.

Parliament Square, adjacent to the cathedral, is home to **Parliament House.** After its construction in 1639, it held sessions of the Scottish Parliament until the "Act of Union" in 1707, but since the 19th century it has been an integral part of the Scottish Law Courts. You'll see solicitors (lawyers) walking the alleyways and streets around the building, carrying briefs in hand and adorned by wigs and capes.

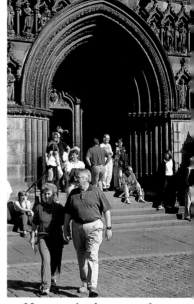

Many tourists have passed beneath the arches of historic St. Giles Cathedral.

Between the cathedral and the High Street entrance to the courts is the **Mercat Cross.** The first cross erected here, in the 14th century, marked the heart of the marketplace and provided a place for royal proclamations to be given a public hearing. It was also a place of execution. The present cross, erected in 1756, is the starting point for many walking tours of the Old Town.

Across High Street you will find the old **Royal Exchange,** built in the 1750s, which was taken over by the town council for Edinburgh's City Chambers in 1811. The chambers stand on the site of St. Mary's Close, an old tenement abandoned in the mid-17th century after the entire population had been wiped out by bubonic plague. The close can still be seen beneath the present buildings, and guided tours are available despite the area's reputation as a spot haunted by victims of the disease. If you take an evening tour, be prepared! Next to the chambers, **Anchor Close** was once home to the printing works of William Smellie, editor and printer of the first edition of the *Encyclopaedia Britannica,* which appeared in 1768.

Continuing down High Street, you will walk past several stores selling highland dress and cashmere before you reach **John Knox House,** on the left side of the road. Said to be the

> **In his writings, John Knox proposed a nation-wide system of education for Scotland to promote universal literacy — a radical idea for the times.**

oldest dwelling house in the city, it dates from 1490. John Knox was a tenant here from 1651 to 1672, but the house was owned by James Mosman, a royal goldsmith, and his wife Mariota Arres; a plaque bearing their initials can be seen on the outer wall. Opened as a museum in 1853, the small rooms display Knox memorabilia and the influential manuscripts from which he preached his Calvinist texts.

Directly across High Street from Knox House is the **Museum of Childhood,** said to be the noisiest museum in the world. Dedicated to games and toys of yesteryear, it is perhaps more suited to adults than children. You'll find many amusing exhibits of street games, clockwork figures, dolls, and teddy bears to bring back memories of your own youth. The museum also has an interesting gift shop featuring toys of all types.

Canongate

The Royal Mile becomes **Canongate** where it intersects St. Mary's Street. This is the former boundary of the town of

Edinburgh and the neighboring town, called Canongate, which was a community of aristocrats and members of the royal court serving Holyrood Palace. The two towns were united in 1856. Canongate derived its name from an edict by David I (1124–1157), founder of the Abbey of Holyrood, who granted a right to raise a gate between the abbey and the Royal "burgh" of Edinburgh.

Several historical buildings lead off Canongate, and a number have interesting stories to tell. **Chessel's Land,** on the left, was the place where Deacon Brodie was finally caught in 1788. **Old Playhouse Close** was

The John Knox house can be found on the Royal Mile. It is now a museum.

the site of a theater where performances resulted in so many riots that it was closed in 1767, after only 20 years. Dating from around 1625, **Moray House** saw a visit from Oliver Cromwell, Lord Protector of England; the house stayed in the Moray family until the mid-19th century.

On the left as you walk, you will see the **Canongate Tolbooth,** with its distinctive clocktower overhanging the pavement. The building on the site dates from 1591 and served as a council chamber and courthouse for the town in addition to collecting tolls. Today the Tolbooth houses **The People's Story,** a museum charting the history of the ordinary folk of the city from the 18th century to the present day. Reconstructions of workshops, pubs, and family rooms show how people lived in previous eras, augmented by written and oral testimonies from townsfolk and a 20-minute introductory video.

Facing the Tolbooth is **Huntly House Museum**, the local history museum for the city, presenting exhibits dating from prehistoric times to the present. The house itself dates from the 16th century. Inside you can find a model of the city as it appeared at that time, as well as the National Covenant document signed by leading Scottish churchmen to protest the attempt by Charles I to introduce Episcopacy (Church of England doctrine) to Scotland. On a more mundane but equally fascinating level, you will see the collar and bowl of "Greyfriars Bobby" (see page 57). Behind Huntly House is Acheson House, home to the **Scottish Craft Centre.**

Nearby **Canongate Church** was built in 1688, and the churchyard has a number of famous "residents." Buried here

are the economist Adam Smith, the poet Robert Ferguson, and Mrs. Agnes McLehose (the "Clarinda" of Burns's love poems).

As the gates of Holyrood Palace come into view, **Whitehorse Close** can be seen on the left. This was the site of the White Horse Inn, the main coaching house at the end of the London–Edin-

Check the clock at the top of the Toll Booth Museum — is it time for lunch?

burgh route. On the right you will see the new Scottish Parliament Building, construction of which began in 1999, and beyond the museum Our Dynamic Earth.

Holyrood

Cross the busy road at the bottom of Canongate to enter the **Holyrood** area, Edinburgh's current royal quarter. It comprises the palace, abbey, and park along with their historic attractions. The easternmost stretch of the Royal Mile — only 50 m- (55 yards-) long — is called Abbey Strand. It is flanked by a building that protected aristocratic debtors (known as the Abbey Lairds) from arrest and certain imprisonment; civil authorities had no jurisdiction within the Abbey grounds and could not enter to arrest them.

Palace of Holyroodhouse

The **Palace of Holyroodhouse** is the official residence in Scotland of the reigning British monarch. However, it began life with a totally different purpose. In 1128 the king, David I, ceded land to the Augustinian order for the creation of the Abbey of Holyrood. The name *Holyrood* means "holy cross" (the Scottish word for "cross" is *rood),* and it is suggested that it is derived from the fact that David gave the abbey a cross that had been owned by his mother, Queen Margaret (later St. Margaret).

Legend gives us a different account: When David was hunting in the woods, he was about to be attacked by a stag when the figure of a cross appeared between the antlers of the beast, which backed away from the king. David gave funds to build an abbey on this site in the depths of the forest in gratitude for his survival.

With its detailed carvings, the beautiful abbey was an important center of worship but continued to have royal

45

connections because of the surrounding hunting grounds. The royal entourage needed some form of lodging, and a guesthouse was built adjoining the abbey to be used as a base for hunting parties.

Scottish kings came to favor the site, and it was James IV who decided to transform the simple lodgings into a true royal palace. In 1501 he had plans drawn up, which his son James V expanded after his death in 1513. In 1529 work started on a tower and royal apartments for James and his wife, Mary of Guise, which now constitute the western section and tower of the current palace. Mary, Queen of Scots, later occupied apartments here, and there are decorative friezes in the rooms from that time.

The lavish landscape of the Palace of Holyroodhouse is probably not maintained by Her Majesty the Queen.

In 1544 the English invaded, set fire to the palace, and sacked the abbey. The great tower, however, survived. It was refurbished and the whole palace greatly extended in the following years. Early in 1650 Oliver Cromwell stationed his garrison here while attempting to subdue the rebellious Scottish monarchists; he was victorious at the Battle of Dunbar. Later that year another devastating fire destroyed much of the structure — though not the tower — and Cromwell made funds available to rebuild the structure. But both the design and workmanship were considered poor.

Following the return of the British monarchy in 1660, Cromwell's work was redone and the buildings extended. Charles II never saw the palace on which he lavished so much money (the royal coffers expended £57,000, a fortune at the time), but he created the foundation of what we see today, with its amazing ornamental plaster work and carved wood paneling. His heir James VI lived at the castle in the 1680s, when the paint was barely dry.

During the 18th century Holyrood was neglected by succeeding British monarchs, who preferred to stay in their London residence, though Scottish noble families lived within the compound. It was not until 1822, when George IV made a state visit, that the fortunes of the palace revived. Since then, almost every reigning monarch has spent time (or held soirées) at Holyrood. The palace has been carefully tended throughout the 20th century.

Visitors can tour the palace only when the monarch is not in residence. Queen Elizabeth will usually spend time in early August, but you should check with tourist authorities if Holyrood is a must-see for you. Helpful guides take you down the long corridors and through the most interesting rooms.

The **Great Stair** is the formal approach to the royal apartments in the southwestern tower. The plaster ceilings here date from 1678 and depict angels carrying the symbols of royal power: crown, scepter, sword, and wreath of laurel leaves. The **Royal Dining Room** is situated at the top of the Great Stair. This majestic room is used for modern-day entertaining when the queen hosts dinners and banquets. On the walls are portraits of Bonnie Prince Charlie and his brother, Prince Henry.

The **Throne Room** is one of a series of apartments built during the reign of Charles II, though it was originally designed as a guard room that screened entrants to the private chambers beyond. The thrones on view here date from a visit by George V and Queen Mary in 1927.

Two magnificent state rooms follow, both designed by Sir William Bruce as part of the extensions and refurbishment in the 1660s. The **Evening and Morning Drawing Rooms** (originally the Presence Chamber and the Privy Chamber) were designed to meet visiting dignitaries and are splendid in their detail; the oak-paneled ceiling is superbly decorated. Be sure to take a look at the painting above the mantle. The scene, depicting Cupid and Psyche, was considered too risqué for the eyes of Queen Victoria, and during her reign it

Holyrood's Grisly Happening

It was a Saturday evening in March 1566. In a small supper room in the west turret, a small group of people were playing cards with Mary, Queen of Scots. Among them were her secretary and favorite, David Rizzio, of whom the queen's husband, Lord Darnley, had become intensely jealous.

Suddenly, a group of Protestants led by Darnley burst into the room and — while the pregnant queen was restrained — dragged Rizzio away to a nearby room, where they stabbed him to death in a frenzied attack. Accounts claim he had over 50 wounds to his body.

was covered by a mirror. The **King's Antechamber** was where he entertained his more favored guests.

Next is the **King's Bedchamber,** perhaps the most richly decorated room in the royal apartments. Seventeenth-century tapestries depicting heroic scenes from the life of Alexander the Great adorn the walls. Although the bed dates from the 1680s, it has never been slept in by royalty. It belongs to the Hamilton family, who have served as hereditary keepers of the palace. Beyond this is the **King's Closet,** where only his intimate entourage would be admitted for evenings of drinking and card games.

From the king's apartments you will enter the

Guided tours are offered at Holyroodhouse when the Queen is not at home.

Great Gallery, a long room that is home to 89 portraits of Scottish rules dating back to antiquity. Commissioned by Charles II, the paintings were all the work of one man, Dutch artist Jacob de Wit. De Wit worked from likenesses of actual monarchs to produce his portraits. For ancient or legendary kings such as Fergus — who was said to have been related to the Pharaohs of Egypt — fashionable imagery of the time helped to create the finished figures.

Make the trek around the winding footpaths encircling Arthur's Seat on your way to conquering the rugged peak.

De Wit was paid a reasonable stipend of £120 per year to produce the works, examples of which can also be seen in other rooms of the palace.

The oldest part of the palace, the **James V Tower** (once called the Great Tower), is for many the highlight of the tour. Its strong stone walls, which survived both fires in the 16th century, sheltered rooms that were occupied by Mary Stuart and her second husband, Lord Darnley, in the 1560s. On the third floor is the **Bed Chamber of Mary, Queen of Scots,** with her antechambers surrounding it. A set of stairs connects her room to that occupied by her husband.

Nearby is the **Outer Chamber of Mary, Queen of Scots,** where she socialized with her favorites and debated religion with John Knox. It is also where her secretary, David Rizzio, was left to bleed to death after being stabbed by Lord Darnley and his cronies; a bronze plaque marks the spot. You will find a number of Mary's personal effects on display. The chambers were totally refurbished by Charles II, including larger windows to balance the design of the new extensions. However, the original ceiling of Mary's bedchamber is still in place.

Abbey of Holyrood and the Park

Outside, set in manicured gardens, are the remains of the **Abbey of Holyrood.** Today it comprises little more than the walls of the church nave. The rest of the abbey was raised to the ground in 1570, but the church was saved because it was a parish church and therefore served the local community. Ornate carvings on the stone façade can still just be discerned, though they have suffered greatly through weathering and pollution. A small stone tomb in the southeast corner houses the bones of several members of the royal family. Originally, these all had separate burial sites, but they were sacked by religious protesters. Queen Victoria arranged for the bones of David II, James II, James V, and Lord Darnley to be re-interred in a common tomb.

To the south of the palace are the green landscapes of **Holyrood Park,** including the volcanic peak known as **Arthur's Seat.** Once royal hunting grounds, today these areas are used for open-air events, concerts, and fireworks displays; the park's trees are almost completely gone. On sunny summer days, people picnic and families spend time in the fresh air. The rugged peak of Arthur's Seat, 251 m (823 ft) in height, can be reached by footpaths all around its base. The path nearest the palace takes walkers along the base of **Salisbury Crags,** a volcanic ridge. The views from the summit of Arthur's Seat — nobody is quite sure which Arthur gave his name to the hill — offer wonderful views of the city and across the Firth of Forth to the north.

On the far side of Arthur's Seat is **Duddingston Loch,** which operates as a bird sanctuary. **Duddingston Kirk,** near the banks of the loch, is one of the oldest Scottish churches still in regular use, founded in the 12th century. Extensions date from the 17th century, including a watch-tower erected in the early 1800s to deter body snatchers. On the causeway leading off Old Church Lane is **Prince Charlie's Cottage,** where the "Young Pretender" stayed in 1745 while planning his strategy to defeat the English and retake the British throne.

Back in the city, the **Scottish Parliament Building** overlooks the palace, the park, and Arthur's Seat. The design for the new building was the subject of a competition won by Spanish architect and designer Enric Miralles. Construction began in 1999.

Edinburgh's attractions showcase both ancient historical sites and futuristic architecture.

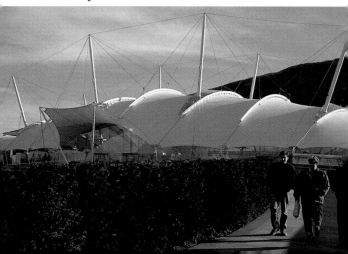

Directly in front of Parliament, on Holyrood Road, is **Our Dynamic Earth,** which opened in July 1999 in a futuristic building under a brilliant white-tented roof. This interactive journey through the history of the earth takes you back to the moment of the "Big Bang." Experience the formation of the continental plates and the development of different climatic regions, then explore the complex and dynamic interactions that make our planet work. The exhibits are entertaining and educational for all age groups, posing questions about our roles as managers of the earth's resources and the future of the planet. The fun parts include getting to touch an iceberg, experiencing the effects of an earthquake in total safety, and lying on the floor of the Showdome to watch exciting weather phenomena flashing above.

Burke and Hare

In the early 18th century, Edinburgh was at the forefront of the medical world, making great strides in the understanding of diseases and infections. As part of this research process, the medical establishment needed cadavers (dead bodies) for dissection, and a grisly black market developed, headed by William Burke and William Hare.

At first they earned their money by digging up freshly buried corpses to sell to physicians, but when demand outstripped supply, they began to roam the streets around the Grassmarket looking for suitable victims, whom they lured into dark alleyways and strangled.

Only when Hare testified in court against his partner was the unsavory business brought to the public eye. Genteel society was outraged. Hare got away with his dastardly deeds, but Burke was hanged in the Grassmarket in 1829 and his body used for medical research.

Grassmarket and Greyfriars

In the shadows of the southern walls of Edinburgh Castle lies the rectangular space of **Grassmarket.** Starting in 1477 this was a marketplace for local farmers as well as one of the main sites for executions in the city. Huge crowds would gather for the gory events — as they did for the markets — and a series of hostelries and pubs set up business to cater to them. Some of these still operate, putting out tables in summer so you can enjoy alfresco drinks and food. Grassmarket has a memorial to the Covenanters (Scottish Protestant clergymen) martyred by Catholic Stuart kings in the 17th century.

From Grassmarket, a road runs parallel to the Royal Mile to Holyrood on a lower level. It has a number of bridges spanning its route, creating a shadowy, dark, and almost somber appearance. The alleyways and passages leading off this main thoroughfare are some of the oldest in the city.

Below Grassmarket is **Cowgate,** known for generations as the Irish Quarter because many families came here to escape the potato famine in their own country. At the western end of Cowgate (where it meets Holyrood Road), you will see one of the few remaining sections of Edinburgh's old city wall (Flodden Wall), built following the "Lang Siege" of the 1570s. In some ways the wall itself was responsible for subsequent overcrowding and disease because people were too frightened to live outside it.

West Bow (said to be so named because it was within a bow's length of the castle walls) and Candlemakers Row are streets leading away from Cowgate Head, at the end of Grassmarket. Here you'll find interesting shops for antiques, collectibles, and antiquarian books. Both these streets lead to the upper level of the George IV Bridge.

Enjoy a sunny afternoon at The Grassmarket, formerly the city's main place for public executions — eek!

From Candlemakers Row, enter the Greyfriars Church-yard through a gate on the right. The **Greyfriars Church** was closely linked with the Protestant Covenanters, and many of those hanged in the Grassmarket are buried here. The church was opened in 1620 — the first one after the Re-formation — and the National Covenant was signed here in 1638. The church became a barracks during Oliver Cromwell's occupation of the city in the 1650; in 1718 there was an explosion of gunpowder that had been stored by city fathers in the tower. Fire did further damage in 1845. Greyfriars Church was restored in 1938 to produce the building you see now.

The graveyard has some extremely ornate and fascinating tombs, replete with skulls and crossbones and other symbols of death. Gravestones rest along the tenement walls marking the outer perimeter. Some of the eminent citizens buried here are George Buchanan, tutor to Mary Queen of Scots; James Craig, architect of Edinburgh's New Town; and Joseph Black, physicist and chemist. You will also find the grave of Greyfriars Bobby, just beside the main entrance. From here you can see some of the most impressive views of the complex layout of the Old Town, with layer upon layer of crenulated rooftops and hundreds of chimneystacks.

The main gate of the churchyard leads out to Greyfriars Place, and across the street you will find an excellent view of one of Scotland's newest museums.

The **Museum of Scotland,** with its main entrance on Chambers Street, is housed in a remarkable new museum building (opened in 1998) designed by architects Benson and

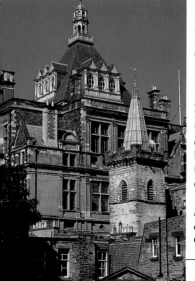

Forsyth. It charts the history of Scotland, bringing under one roof a number of important collections of artifacts. The story begins 3.4 billion years ago with displays of fossils and rock, marking the geological changes that forged the landscape. It continues through the turbulent eras of Scottish history for both church and state, and on to the industrial developments of modern times.

Be sure to notice the regal architecture around the Greyfriars churchyard.

Fascinating details such as Bonnie Prince Charlie's traveling canteen of cutlery, along with his sword and *targe* (a small bag), bring history to life. Exhibits are devoted to Scottish pioneers Sir Alexander Fleming and Alexander Graham Bell, among others. A fine collection of medieval church artifacts and Celtic carvings can be found on the first floor. A roof terrace offers panoramic views over the city skyline, and there is an excellent restaurant on the third floor.

This new museum was built as an annex to the existing **Royal Museum,** a beautiful Victorian edifice with a large glass roof — much like a glass house. The Royal Museum has displays devoted to anthropology, archaeology, natural sciences, and technology. Collections such as Asian art and Egyptian artifacts are on terraced balconies, allowing a full view of the roof from the ground floor. There are always several temporary exhibits to explore, along with a café and gift

---

Greyfriars Bobby

One of the most famous inhabitants of Edinburgh, Greyfriars Bobby was a Skye terrier belonging to "Auld Jock" Gray, a local police constable. When Jock died in 1858, Bobby followed the funeral procession to the graveyard at Greyfriars Church and then stayed at his master's grave for the next fourteen years, leaving it only to look for food at the nearby tavern.

Though he was legally a stray and thus under threat of being destroyed, the whole city rallied around the faithful dog. The Lord Provost issued a license that allowed Bobby to maintain his vigil, which he did until his death in 1873. He was buried in the graveyard, with a statue financed by public donations and erected outside the tavern. Bobby's collar and bowl can be seen at Huntly House Museum, and his story is told in a Walt Disney movie.

shop. Tickets for the Museum of Scotland allow entrance also to the main collections of the Royal Museum, fulfilling the stated aim of the curators of "bringing Scotland to the world, and the world to Scotland."

The two museums are at the heart of the old **University of Edinburgh** quarter, with students still attending lectures in the sandstone buildings. Although the campus has grown and now occupies sites all around the city, the streets here have cheap eateries, stores selling eclectic clothing, and bookstores; James Thin, on South Bridge, is the largest bookstore in the city.

South of the museum, a short walk down Forest Road brings you to the **Edinburgh Royal Infirmary.** The city has a long-standing international reputation for research and development, which began in 1681 with the founding of the Royal College of Physicians. The School of Medicine followed only a few years later. The first infirmary was founded in 1737; in 1805 the *Edinburgh Medical and Surgical Journal* was the first in the world published to promote discussion and knowledge of medicine. Joseph Lister pioneered the use of carbolic acid to keep wounds clean, and James Young Simpson experimented with chloroform as an anesthetic.

Opposite the infirmary, with an entrance on Lauriston Place, is the ornate **George Heriot School.** Although not open to the public, its towers and beautifully carved stone walls can be seen from various vantage points in the city. It has an interesting story to tell. George Heriot was banker, goldsmith, and jeweler to James IV. When he died in 1624, he bequeathed his fortune to the education and upkeep of orphans, and the school was subsequently built for this purpose.

THE NEW TOWN

By the beginning of the 18th century, life in the city of Edinburgh (today's Old Town) was overcrowded and unsan-

New Town is not really all that new — construction began in the 18th century — but it is worth a visit.

itary. The city had grown very little since the 14th century, yet its population was said to be over 50,000. Large families lived in high tenements, sharing a well with hundreds of other families. Sewage and dirty water were thrown from upper floors to the streets below and left to fester.

In 1725 the provost of the city, George Drummond, first raised the possibility of expansion to the northeast, across what was called Barefoot's Parks to the green fields beyond. His ideas were not made official until 1752, and it was another 14 years before plans were put into place for a competition to create a design for this new development, to be called the **New Town.**

There were logistical problems to be overcome. At the foot of the castle was Nor' Loch, a large expanse of water that required draining. There would also have to be adequate access between the older and newer parts of town, including a bridge over the valley between Barefoot's Parks and the Royal Mile. The prize for the competition winner was a gold medal — along with world fame.

The winner, announced in 1766, was James Craig, an unknown 23-year-old architect and native of the city. His plan was a simple grid: a symmetrical design with straight streets and grand squares. The recent union with England was the inspiration for street names such as "Rose" and "Thistle." Craig also praised the royal family with George Street, Queen Street, and Princes Street. Surprisingly, the plan contained little detail for the buildings that would line the streets and frame the squares. Instead, Craig concentrated on the overall design.

In 1763 construction had already begun on North Bridge, which would provide access from the Old Town. Nor' Loch was drained (creating land for today's Princes Street Gardens), and the Mound was constructed to provide a second, westerly access between the two settlements. Initial demand for land in the New Town was not spectacular; in fact, incentives had to be offered to entice buyers.

The first houses built here did not adhere to any set design. In 1782, after only a few years, the city decided to impose planning guidelines. At the same time, an architect named

Is There a Doctor in the House?

The city's first woman doctor earned her degree in 1812. But because of the strict separation of the sexes at the time, women were not allowed to receive professional qualifications. "James" Barry made the decision to live her life as a man. Her gender was revealed only when the autopsy was carried out after her death.

Robert Adam became popular in the fashionable circles of the well-to-do, having made a name for himself in England. It was he who would add the "flesh" of handsome buildings to the "bones" of Craig's design.

By the beginning of the 19th century, the New Town had become so popular that plans were made for a second stage. This would be a largely residential area extending north from Queen Street, incorporating a number of traffic circles (circuses) as well as straight roads. Most influential at this stage was architect William Playfair, and his flair can be seen in many of the streets and public buildings of the time. These streets are still largely residential and make an interesting area to stroll, displaying a wealth of original detail. Edinburgh became known as the "Athens of the North" for both its aesthetic beauty and its wealth of talented individuals. Notable artists, writers, philosophers, and scientists seemed to flock to the city.

> **When crossing streets, look first to the right for traffic and then to the left.**

Today the streets of the New Town have perhaps the greatest collection of Georgian architecture in the world. Many areas enjoy protected status to save them for future generations to enjoy. Because so many buildings are still residences, however, there are relatively few attractions to visit compared with the Old Town.

Princes Street

Looking north from the high ground of the Old Town, the first street you can see is **Princes Street.** It was once regarded as the most beautiful street in Europe, a claim that is difficult to understand today since so many of the original buildings have been replaced. Princes Street is to Scots what Oxford Street is to the English — the premier shopping street of the land. Wide walkways have plenty of room for shoppers, and there are splendid views of the castle all along its length.

On the south side of the street — in the open ground below the castle and on the site of the formerly marshy Nor' Loch — are **Princes Street Gardens,** a welcome place to relax in a sunny day. The West Gardens have a number of interesting memorial statues and sculptures, including the **Scottish American War Memorial** and the **Royal Scots Memorial.**

An the center of the gardens is **Ross Open Air Bandstand,** which plays host to free concerts throughout the year, particularly during the festival season. During the summer, beside the flight of steps carrying people up to the Mound, you will find the **Floral Clock.** Planted with hundreds of pretty blooms, all in pristine condition, it has kept accurate time since its creation in 1903.

The National Gallery of Scotland is home to works by Gauguin, Pouissin, Raphael, and other renowned artists.

The West and East Gardens are split by the **Mound,** an artificial slope of rock and soil that carries a road connecting the New Town with the Old. Here you will find two of the most important galleries in the city, housed in classical buildings designed by Playfair. Set back from Princes Street is the **National Gallery of Scotland,** opened in 1858, which houses a collection of works by native Scottish artists and international masters. The collection — and indeed the building itself — is not huge or overbearing, allowing visitors to relax and enjoy the art perhaps more than is possible in such massive galleries as the Louvre or Rijksmuseum. Initially known as the Royal Institute in the 1830s, the National Gallery benefited from a number of bequests, not least that of the Duke of Sutherland in 1946. In 1995 the gallery and London's Victoria and Albert Museum jointly purchased *The Three Graces,* a sculpture by Antonio Canova that was in danger of being sold abroad.

What it lacks in size, the gallery makes up for in quality. Works such as Raphael's *Bridgewater Madonna,* a Rembrandt *Self-Portrait,* and Velázquez's *Old Woman Cooking Eggs* are only three from a collection that includes pieces by Titian, Van Dyck, Rubens, Constable, Turner, and Vermeer. Scottish artists include Allan Ramsey, Sir Henry Raeburn, and Sir David Wilkie.

In front of the National Gallery is the **Royal Scottish Academy** building, designed as almost its twin. It holds regular exhibits and displays by academy members.

Between the two buildings, **East Princes Gardens** are smaller than the West Gardens. In winter a large ice rink covers the lawns, where you can enjoy outdoor skating in a picturesque setting. Rising above the flower beds is the solemn **Scott Monument,** complete with a resident flock of pigeons that badger people on surrounding park benches for crumbs. The Scott Monument is a huge, stone Gothic structure with four buttresses supporting a spire. The whole edifice is 61 m (200 ft) high. In its shadow sits the statue of novelist Sir Walter Scott (and his faithful dog, Maida) carved from Cararra marble. Designed by George Meikle Kemp, an unknown draftsman of humble birth, the monument took its inspiration from the design of Melrose Abbey. Sixty-four additional statuettes carved into the structure represent characters from Scott's books. Steps inside the outer columns lead up to galleries at four levels, and the view from the top gallery is spectacular.

> Livingstone died in Africa in 1873 after exploring more of that continent than any other European. He named the Zambezi River's Victoria Falls after Britain's monarch.

A small garden to the west of the Scott Monument has a memorial to David Livingstone, the explorer and missionary. Created by Amelia Hill, it is the only statue in the garden to have been sculpted by a woman. When it was unveiled, it received much criticism because many thought it too small to occupy an open space.

Beyond the two monuments is Waverley Bridge. Here you can pick up buses for a tour of city attractions. This is also the site of **Waverley Station,** and the sound of arriving trains can be heard as background noise throughout the day. The lines take a dramatic route through ditches cut through Princes Street Gardens and under the Mound (in the National Gallery you can feel a faint movement as the trains travel underneath). Waverley Street Shopping Centre, which sits on the corner of Princes Street, is where you will find the main Tourist Information Office.

On the south side of the station is Market Street, which was one of the principle market sites during the Victorian era. Market Street is home to the **Edinburgh City Art Gallery,** showcasing the work of up-and-coming artists. On the same street you will also find the ticket office for the Military Tattoo (see pages 35), with an accompanying gallery and souvenir shop.

At the eastern end of Princes Street is **Register House,** completed in 1788 from a design by Robert Adam and built for the Scottish public records office. Today it stores land-registry papers and is the haunt of solicitors and professional researchers. In front of the building is a

The Scott Monument is a Gothic masterpiece not to be missed!

statue of the Duke of Wellington, resplendent in battle dress and cloak astride his trusty steed, Copenhagen.

George Street

George Street was the centerpiece of Craig's original design for the New Town. The grand thoroughfare, anchored at each end by a large square, had a symmetrical pattern of streets on both its flanks.

George Street was the traditional center of Edinburgh's financial district. Behind the strong, plain, painted doors, many successful bankers increased the wealth of their trusting investors. Scottish banking has long been held in high regard, and it still plays an important part in the world of finance. However, the buildings — beautiful though they are — have not been able to accommodate modern computerized banking equipment; increasingly, the institutions have moved to modern buildings around the city. This doesn't make George Street an empty shell. Where banks have moved out, fashionable wine bars and restaurants have moved in, making it a great place to come for drinks or dinner.

☞ The western end of George Street begins at **Charlotte Square,** originally named St. George's Square after the patron saint of England (mirroring St. Andrew's Square at the street's eastern end, which was named for the patron saint of Scotland). The name was changed to honor Queen Charlotte — George III's wife — who felt a little upset at having been left out of the original plans. After all, her husband

At the National Portrait Gallery, you can get to know Scotland's rich and complex history.

and two sons had roads named after them: George Street and Princes Street.

Charlotte Square is arguably the jewel of the New Town. The façades of elegant houses on the north side were designed by Adam and have changed little since they were finished in 1805. In the center of the terrace is **Georgian House,** owned by the National Trust and restored in period style to show the workings of a typical Georgian household. All of the many pieces in the house are authentic, including a huge array of kitchen utensils, crockery, cutlery, furniture, carpets, and curtains. Most surprising is the fact that the bed-chamber is on the first floor rather than on the second; upper-floor bedrooms became fashionable only at a later date.

On the western flank of the square, **West Register House,** designed originally as a church (St. George's), was taken over by the government in 1960 and is now part of the Public Records Office. The building at the corner of Charlotte Square and South Charlotte Street was the birthplace of Alexander Graham Bell, inventor of the telephone. Plans are in place to turn the house into a museum charting the life and works of this extraordinary man.

Four streets to the east on George Street, the most stun-ning building on **St. Andrew's Square** is that belonging to the Royal Bank of Scotland. Originally a house, it was designed by Sir William Chambers and completed in 1772; the dome was added in 1858.

Scottish National Portrait Gallery

From St. Andrew's Square, it is only a short walk north to Queen Street, where you will find the **Scottish National Portrait Gallery** on the corner. More than 200 paintings of famous — and infamous — Scots can be found in the collec-tion, which was initiated by David, 11th Earl of Buchan.

Following the earl's death, Scottish historian Thomas Carlyle decided to inspire his fellow countrymen through a national gallery devoted to their heroes. He obtained private backing for the creation of the gallery, which opened in 1889.

Designed by Sir Robert Rowand Anderson, the building was constructed in neo-Gothic style, and statues on the outer façade depict Scottish poets, artists, and statesmen. The entrance hall also portrays famous Scots in a beautifully detailed frieze just below the cornice; it's a veritable "Who's Who" of the Scottish establishment. The entrance is also home to several sculptures, including one of Carlyle, the gallery's founding father.

The galleries are arranged chronologically, which helps put the figures into context. You'll of course see Mary Stuart (Mary, Queen of Scots) and Bonnie Prince Charlie — as

Secret Gardens

Like many cities, Edinburgh has picturesque gardens among its paved streets and rows of houses. Unlike other cities, however, many of these gardens are private and enjoyed by only a favored few.

When the New Town was planned in the 1760s, it incorporated squares (such as St. Andrew's) and green spaces (such as Queen Street Gardens) as an integral part of the design. The gardens were held in common by the householders who lived around them, with each household having a key to gain access through locked, wrought-iron gates.

The rights and responsibilities of the "keyholders" have been passed down through the generations, and today these gates are still locked to the general public. The fine statues and manicured lawns may be viewed from the outside only.

himself and also as Betty Burke, his disguise to escape the English forces. Sir Walter Scott and Robert Adam are here, but you will also find individuals such as Neil Gow, a virtuoso fiddler of great renown in his own lifetime (1727–1807). Likenesses can be found on canvas, on bronze or plaster "medals," or as sculptures. There is an interesting section devoted to 20th-century Scots, including Queen Elizabeth (the Queen Mother), who was born at Glamis Castle in 1900. The gallery also has a strong policy of both acquiring and commissioning works depicting modern Scots in the public eye (including actors Sean Connery and Robbie Coltrane and Manchester United football manager Sir Alex Ferguson), which keeps its exhibitions fresh and fulfills Carlyle's original aims.

Calton Hill

From the eastern end of Princes Street, the eye is drawn to a hill topped with a series of interesting albeit disparate buildings. This is **Calton Hill,** built around 100 m (328 ft) of hard volcanic rock, and its monuments and architecture are said to have been responsible for Edinburgh's epithet "Athens of the North." You will be met

For a small fee, climb to the top of the towering Nelson Monument.

by a flight of steep steps, but the superb views across the city make the climb worthwhile.

At the very crest of the hill, you will find the Old Observatory, the only building designed by James Craig left in the city; it was completed in 1792. An additional observatory was added in the 1820s, but the smoky skies and train steam over the city at that time made it an unsuitable location for watching the stars. The Royal Observatory was relocated to Blackford Hill, farther south, in 1895. Today the old building hosts the **Edinburgh Experience,** a 20-minute, 3-D slide show charting the history of the city and bringing to life the Edinburgh of today (April–October only).

The nearby **Nelson Monument,** an elegant tower 30 m (98 ft) high, commemorates the famous naval victory at Trafalgar in 1805. You can climb the column for magnificent views of the city and the Firth of Forth to the north. At the top of the tower is a white ball on a metal stake. As one o'clock approaches, the ball rises to the top of the stake and then drops exactly on the stroke of one. This device is a visual counterpart to the firing of the One O'Clock Gun at the Castle. It could easily be seen by ships in the Firth of Forth and was a useful safeguard if prevailing winds carried the sound of the gunfire the wrong way.

A colonnaded circular monument to the right was raised in the memory of Dugald Stewart, professor of moral philosophy at the University of Edinburgh in the 1780s. The classical design was taken from examples in Athens.

The most fascinating structure on Calton Hill is the **National Monument.** What looks from a distance like a huge Greek temple with many Ionic columns turns out to be only a single façade with 12 columns. It was planned in the 1820s as a symbol of Scottish national pride and

It may be known as "Scotland's Disgrace," but the National Monument is still worth a visit when atop Carlton Hill.

designed as a mini-Parthenon, in deference to the neoclassical style popular at the time. Unfortunately, the public was not enthusiastic, the funding ran out, and the project was abandoned, giving the monument its other name: "Scotland's Disgrace."

EDINBURGH'S VILLAGES

Edinburgh has throughout most of its history been a very compact city. Even the New Town had very set boundaries. The entire city was surrounded by open countryside with a scattering of small villages. But massive growth during the 20th century saw Edinburgh absorb many of these formerly independent communities into its ever-enlarging limits. Surprisingly — and happily — the villages did not allow their character to be diluted and swallowed up into one homogenous suburb. They still maintain their own individual charms and are certainly an important element in Edinburgh's continuing appeal.

Dean Village

Less than one kilometer (half a mile) from the western end of Princes Street is **Dean Village.** It is set on the ribbon-thin Water of Leith, whose narrow valley drops steeply here. Dean Bridge carries the main road over the Water; it was designed and built by Thomas Telford, one of Scotland's greatest civil engineers.

Dean was an industrial village, its economy depending on numerous small mills that have now completely disappeared. A walk beside the Water offers the most interesting views, so don't cross the bridge. Instead, take the cobbled alley of Bells Brae to Hawthornbank Road, down in the valley. You'll see fascinating views of the rear of the Georgian houses of the New Town as well as the small cottages of Dean Village itself.

> **Be prepared to stand in lines. Queuing is still expected in Britain.**

 A ten-minute walk east on Belford Road brings you to two important art galleries. The **Scottish National Gallery of Modern Art,** founded in 1959, occupies the site of the former John Watson's School, a neoclassical building dating from the 1820s. The gallery rooms display some of the best in 20th-century art. Cubists are represented by Picasso (including *Mother and Child,* from his Blue Period) and Braque. There are pieces by Matisse, Magritte, Miró, and Hockney. Sculptures inside the gallery include works by Giacometti, and there are several large sculptures by Henry Moore displayed in the surrounding grounds.

Opposite the modern art gallery is the **Dean Gallery,** occupying a fine Victorian mansion that was once an orphanage. The gallery brings together a number of excellent private collections, including works by local Scottish artist Eduardo Paolozzi.

Inverleith

Immediately north of Edinburgh's New Town is **Inverleith,** an area full of green sites. Large schools with acres of grounds, playing fields, and recreation areas are interspersed with sumptuous houses set in leafy lanes. It was here that the **Royal Botanic Garden** was moved in 1823 from a location not far from the Abbey of Holyrood. The garden had been founded as early as 1670 as a resource for medical research, affiliated for many years with the Royal College of Physicians.

The present site covers 28 hectares (70 acres) of ground divided into several different natural environments. The huge Victorian greenhouse, New Palm House, is impressive and packed with ferns and palms that thrive in the warm, damp environment. A large 1960s greenhouse sits beside it and, though lacking the elegance of its neighbor, still boasts an impressive collection. The surrounding landscaped grounds are kept in pristine condition. Mature trees shade lawns and flower beds that are home to numerous birds species and cheeky gray squirrels. You can also wander through the soothing Chinese garden, with its waterfalls and pretty red pergola.

Corstorphine

About 5 km (3 miles) west of Edinburgh's center, past the rugby ground at Murrayfield, you will find **Corstorphine.** For centuries this was a farming village, separated from the

You don't have to wear your tuxedo to the Edinburgh Zoo, but the penguins are always dressed for dinner!

city by the green expanse of Corstorphine Hill. On the slopes of the hill you will find **Edinburgh Zoo,** located just behind Corstorphine Hospital.

The zoo opened in 1913 and was designed with enclosures rather than cages, an idea that was new at the time. This offered a more natural habitat for animals and a clearer view for visitors. When the zoo celebrated the first successful hatching in captivity of a king penguin in 1919, it gained world renown: no other zoo had examples of this penguin species.

Today Edinburgh Zoo continues work on the conservation of animal species and acts as an educational resource. The penguins still take pride of place — the zoo has the world's largest group in captivity — and they take a stroll around the zoo in the "Penguin Parade" every day during the summer (April–October).

There are over 156 species of animals on view here, with notable successes in the breeding of endangered rhinos and Rothschild giraffes. There are also beautiful big cats and a large "Plains of Africa" exhibit, where herds of antelope and zebra graze peacefully in the Scottish sunshine. The zoo lies on a hillside, with visitors needing to climb some inclines to the upper enclosures (wheelchairs and strollers are available).

Leith

Situated on the coast, **Leith** is only 5 km (3 miles) from the city center. It has been an important settlement since the 14th century and was the largest port in Scotland for many years, handling Edinburgh's cargo. It was a fiercely independent settlement with its own fishing fleet and ship-building industry. In 1920 Leith was incorporated into the city of Edinburgh.

After a brief 20th-century decline, Leith's fortunes have revived. The old warehouses have been transformed into upscale apartments and fashionable office buildings, and there is a buzz of chic commercial activity that has spawned smart restaurants and wine bars. Older locals — trawler men or dockworkers — might lament the loss of Leith's gritty, "salt-of-the-earth" reputation, but the town has an air of excitement about it. Buses from the city center will carry you here in minutes.

In 1997 the ***Royal Yacht Britannia,*** the vessel that carried the queen and her official representatives on 968 royal and diplomatic visits to venues around the world, was decommissioned. The fate of the ship was undecided, and at one time it was thought that it might be scrapped, but eventually it became a tourist attraction. Several cities made bids to host the ship, and Edinburgh's was successful; her new home would be at Leith. After some work to make her visitor-friendly, she lowered her gangplank to the public in October 1998.

The ship was launched in April 1953, when Elizabeth II was in the first few months of her reign. She and her husband, Prince Philip, were very much involved in the interior decoration of the ship, choosing the furnishings for what would be their floating home. The royal quarters have changed little since that time. *Britannia* was the place where the queen said she could truly relax, and it is very much a reflection of her personal taste — surprising for its lack of the ornate trappings that fill her official palaces.

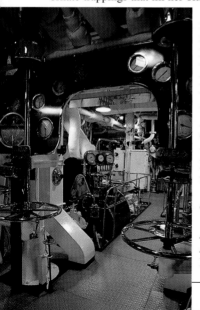

The ship entertained presidents, princes, and diplomats, but most people perhaps remember *Britannia* as the royal honeymoon boat. Princess Margaret began the tradition, to be followed by three of the queen's children: Anne, Andrew, and of course Charles, who journeyed with the newly designated Diana, Princess of Wales, around the Mediterranean in 1981.

The most attractive part of Leith is the **Shore,** a few

Engine Room of the Britannia — once the Royal Yacht to Queen Elizabeth II.

minutes' walk east of *Britannia*. The Shore formed around the mouth of the Waters of Leith, the narrow river running through Edinburgh. Even here the Waters are really little more than a large stream, but they flow into the Firth of Forth and beyond into the North Sea. The Shore comprises a quay-side and several cobbled lanes with restaurants where you can have a pleasant lunch. The surrounding warehouse districts have interesting stores for souvenir browsing. A little way to the south are **Leith Links,** said to be the birthplace of golf, where the Honourable Company of Edinburgh Golfers built a clubhouse in 1767 and where you can still enjoy a bracing round in the sea air.

Cramond

At present-day **Cramond,** located at the mouth of the River Almond, the Romans constructed a fort in the second century A.D., at the eastern end of a defensive structure called the Antonine Wall. The foundations of the fort can still be seen, but artifacts from the site are displayed in the Huntly House Museum in Edinburgh.

Sailboats and small pleasure craft dock at Cramond, where the tidal river exits into the Firth of Firth. Much of the village is from the 18th century, and the whitewashed cottages are very picturesque. There are pleasant walks along the coastline and stops for refreshment at the Cramond Inn, which is believed to be a setting described in Robert Louis Stevenson's *St. Ives.*

Portobello

With its wide, sandy beach, **Portobello** is a quintessential British seaside town. When bathing in the sea became popular at the end of the 18th century, wealthy families from Edinburgh began to spend days here "taking the waters" in state-of-the art "bathing machines." In summer you can come to dip your feet in the sea and treat yourself to an ice cream or cotton candy; in spring or fall, enjoy a bracing stroll in the sea air.

EXCURSIONS

If you have a few days to explore the region, you'll find a wealth of things to see nearby. The Edinburgh and Lothians Tourist Board produces automobile tours for East Lothian, West Lothian, and Midlothian, with suggested itineraries, opening times, and prices for various sights and attractions.

Queensferry and the Forth Bridge

Approximately 13 kilometers (8 miles) west of the city is **Queensferry,** a town that developed as a crossing point of the Firth of Forth for routes to the north of Scotland. It is said that Queen Margaret, later Saint Margaret, traveled this route regularly in the late 11th century and that the town took its name from her journeys. A plaque on the water's edge at the Binks (a natural jetty formed by a rocky outcrop) marks her landing site.

The old water ferry no longer runs, but Queensferry remains the crossing point for modern-day travelers in their motorized machines. The logistical problems of spanning the Firth were numerous, but their solution resulted in one of the greatest engineering achievements of the Victorian era, the **Forth Railway Bridge.** Completed in 1890, the bridge comprises three huge cantilevers joined by two suspended spans, for a total length of 1,447 m (4,746 ft). For many years it was the longest bridge in the world, and the huge structure seems to overshadow the town, which sits on the banks of the river below. Maintenance is a mammoth task, and it is said that painters work constantly on the structure, completing one end and immediately starting again at the other.

In 1964 a sister structure, the **Forth Road Bridge,** was completed to take vehicular traffic across the Firth. The bridge is a single, unsupported span 1,006 m (3,300 ft) in length. Fascinating pictures of the construction of both bridges can be found in the town museum on Queensferry's High Street.

Take a stroll around the picture-perfect little fishing harbor, where the boats become stranded like beached whales at low tide. From a small jetty below the railway bridge, you can take a ferry out into the Firth of Forth to tiny **Inchcolm Island.** Here you'll find the ruined Abbey of St. Colm,

The tall masts at the Queensferry yacht harbor offset the majestic symmetry of the Forth rail bridge.

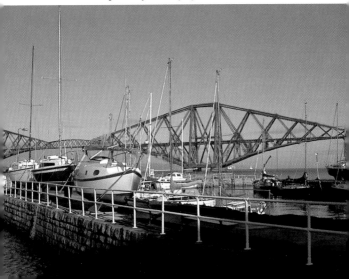

Completed in 1890, the Forth Railway Bridge is still a marvel to behold.

founded in the 12th century and named for St. Columba, who had brought Christianity to western Scotland 600 years earlier. You can also watch the playful antics of the small colony of seals that call the island home.

Edinburgh Crystal

Twenty minutes southwest of the city by car is the small town of **Penicuik**. It is an unremarkable place save for its most important product. This is the home of fine Edinburgh crystal, one of the most recognizable and beautiful souvenirs of a stay in the city.

The **Edinburgh Crystal Factory** has guided tours that show every aspect of the production of cut lead glassware. You'll see the hot furnaces where the glass mixture (the batch) is melted and blown, and you'll watch the cutting that is done by hand and eye as well as the polishing or engraving. Edinburgh Crystal has an excellent retail store on site and a factory shop where "second-quality" goods are sold. They sell tax-free goods for travelers from outside the EU, with shipping arranged on site. If you don't have transportation, Edinburgh Crystal operates a shuttle bus service to and from the center of Edinburgh.

Museums, Galleries, and Attractions

Camera Obscura: Castlehill. Open daily Nov–Mar 10am–5pm, Apr–Jun and Sept–Oct 9:30am–6pm, Jul–Aug 9:30am–7pm. Admission: £3.95

Dean Gallery: Belford Street. Open daily 10am–5pm. Admission: adult £4 (children under 12 free).

Edinburgh Castle: Open daily Apr–Sept 9:30am–6pm, Oct–Mar 9:30am–5pm. Admission: adult £6.50, child £2.

Edinburgh Military Tattoo: Edinburgh Castle Esplanade. Month of August only (dates vary), nightly except Sunday. Admission £11–£25 (tickets: 32 Market Street).

Edinburgh Zoo: Corstorphine Road. Open daily Apr–Sept 9am–6pm, Oct and Mar 9am–5pm, Nov–Feb 9am–4:30pm. Admission: adult £6.80, children aged 3–14 £3.80.

Georgian House: Charlotte Square. Open Apr–Oct, Monday–Saturday 10am–5pm, Sunday 2pm–5pm. Admission: adult £4.40, child £2.90.

Huntly House Museum: Canongate. Open Monday–Saturday 10am–5pm, Sunday during the festival 2pm–5pm. Admission free.

Museum of Childhood: High Street. Open Monday–Saturday 10am–5pm, Sunday during the festival 2pm–5pm. Admission free.

Museum of Scotland and **Royal Museum**: Chambers Street. Open Monday–Saturday 10am–5pm, Tuesday until 10pm, Sunday noon–5pm. Admission: adult £3, child £1.50.

National Gallery of Modern Art: Belford Street. Open Monday–Saturday 10am–5pm, Sunday 2pm–5pm. Admission free.

National Gallery of Scotland: the Mound. Open Monday–Saturday 10am–5pm, Sunday 2pm–5pm. Admission free.

Nelson's Column: Calton Hill. Open Apr–Sep Monday–Saturday 10am–6pm, Oct–Mar Monday–Saturday 10am–3pm. Admission: £2.00.

Our Dynamic Earth: Holyrood Road. Open Easter–Nov daily 10am–6pm, Nov–Easter Wednesday–Sunday 10am–5pm. Admission: adult £5.95, child £3.50.

Palace of Holyroodhouse: Holyrood. Open daily except when royalty is in residence, Apr–Oct 9:30am–5:15pm, Nov–Mar 9:30am–3:45pm. Admission: adult £6, child £2.70.

The People's Story: Canongate Tolbooth. Open Monday–Saturday 10am–5pm, Sunday during the festival 2pm–5pm. Admission free.

Royal Yacht Britannia: Ocean Drive, Leith. Open daily 10:30am–4:30pm (later in summer). Reservations advisable, tickets available from the Britannia Visitors Centre or at the Edinburgh Tattoo Office, 32 Market St., Edinburgh. Admission: adult £7.50, child £3.75.

Scott Monument: Princes Street. Open May–Oct daily 10am–6pm; Jun–Sep Monday–Saturday 10am–6pm, Nov–Feb Monday–Saturday 10am–4pm. Admission: £2.50.

Scottish National Portrait Gallery: Queen Street. Open Monday–Saturday 10am–5pm, Sunday 2pm–5pm. Admission free.

Scottish Whisky Heritage Centre: Castlehill. Open daily 10am–5:30pm (extended hours in summer). Admission: adult £7.50, children aged 5–17 £2.75.

St. Giles Cathedral: High Street. Open daily except during special services. Admission free.

Writers' Museum: Lady Stair's House, Lady Stair's Close, Lawnmarket. Open Monday–Saturday 10am–5pm, Sunday during the festival 2pm–5pm. Admission free.

WHAT TO DO

ENTERTAINMENT

Edinburgh's Festivals

Although Edinburgh has many year-round attractions, the city bursts into life in July, August, and early September with a number of separate festivals running concurrently. The major festivals discussed below are joined by the Film Festival, the Jazz and Blues Festival, and the Book Festival (said to be the biggest public book fair in the world). The city almost bursts at the seams as up to 500,000 visitors arrive, vying for street space with performers, clowns, face painters, and numerous small craft markets. For additional information, you can access websites for all the festivals at <www.edinburghfestivals.co.uk> (see TICKETS, page 127, for contact information for the various festivals).

Edinburgh International Festival

In 1947 Edinburgh hosted its first International Festival. With the talent of impresario Rudolf Bing, it was a great success and rapidly became one of the premier festivals of its kind in the world. Every year, for three weeks in August and September, all eyes are on the dozens of performances and events in the many theaters of the city center. Although the first festival was biased toward orchestral music, the modern festival has a comprehensive program of dance, music, opera, and theater, with some of the finest exponents in every field gracing the stage. Over the years Trevor Howard, Margot Fonteyn, and Marlene Dietrich brought their own inimitable style to the festival. Details of the International Festival program are available in March each year.

Edinburgh Festival Fringe

The Festival Fringe was born at the same time as the official festival and acts as a sometimes irreverent, loose collection of extra performances held in the city. Initially the Fringe consisted of several small theater companies that were not included in the official festival program but nevertheless decided to hold performances on the same dates.

Free from the confines of the International Festival's rules and regulations, the Fringe has become synonymous with art that "pushes the envelope," and it has grown to eclipse its more staid official brother. It comprises over 1500 different shows, with literally dozens of performances taking place daily (at all times of the day and night). Venues have included the front seat of a car — where the small audience sat in the back!

Toward the end of August, behold the street performers of the Festival Fringe.

Performers such as Peter Cook and Dudley Moore made the Fringe their own, and Tom Stoppard's *Rosencrantz and Guildenstern Are Dead* was premiered here. Every year the cream of young artistic and comedic talent makes its way to Edinburgh, and the Fringe has grown into arguably the largest showcase for burgeoning performers in the world. A program is produced in June each year covering the hundreds of Fringe performances, while a daily program is published during the festival itself.

Edinburgh Military Tattoo

In 1950 the city established a Military Tattoo at the same time as the Festival, and the two have now become an inseparable combination. A *tattoo* is a highly polished show of military marching, pageantry, mock battles, and horsemanship, accompanied by the sounds of pipe-and-drum bands from around the world. All this happens nightly (except Sunday) against the backdrop of the magnificently floodlit castle in an arena erected in the Esplanade.

> **A true Scotsman wears nothing under his kilt!**

The Military Tattoo has an office at 32 Market Street and shop/gallery at 33–34 Market Street (behind Waverley Station), where you can see photographs from past events as well as purchase souvenirs and tickets.

Other Entertainment

Hogmanay

The Scots have traditionally hosted "the best New Year celebrations in the world," and Edinburgh has expanded the one night into a five-night Hogmanay Festival of torchlight parades, street theater, and food fair in the days before 31 December (website: <www.edinburghshogmanay.org>). For those who still have some energy left after a night of revels, there is also a New Year's Day triathlon.

Nightlife

Of course you don't need to visit Edinburgh during the summer festivals to see performances of the arts. The city is home to the Scottish Opera and Ballet and the Scottish National Orchestra, among other resident companies. There are also several major theaters with an ever-changing schedule of plays, ballets, and musical performances as well as popular shows featuring international bands and singers on the tour circuit. Although you will find venues scattered throughout the city, the main theater district is found south of the west end of Princes Street.

Whichever month you decide to visit, the Edinburgh and Lothians Tourist Board produces *What's On,* a leaflet to help you make your plans. Also available locally is the magazine *The List,* with complete events for Edinburgh and Glasgow.

Scottish Nights

A number of companies will offer an evening of Scottish dancing along with an "addressing the haggis" ceremony — traditionally performed on Burns Night, the birthday of the poet who wrote an ode to this favorite Scottish dish. You will find all the paraphernalia of kilts, bagpipes, and ceremonial arms along with traditional Scottish food, whisky, and dancing. The Caledonian Brewery holds regular evenings called *ceilidhs* —

a Gaelic word for informal gatherings with music, dance, stories, and song (42 Slateford Road; Tel. 337 1286).

Pubs

Many people can't visit Edinburgh without spending a little time enjoying a glass of beer in a pub. There are many different establish-

Many fine beers are brewed in Edinburgh — try a pint in Deacon Brodies Tavern.

ments to choose from, each with its own clientele and style. Finding one that suits you is all part of the fun. Most will serve snacks during the day, and you may even be able to order a full lunch or evening meal for a bargain price.

For a traditional pub where you can sit among the locals, try the Guildford Arms, on West Register Street one block north of the east end of Princes Street. The brass beer taps and frosted-glass windows are the epitome of pub décor. The Last Drop Pub (on Grassmarket) is another traditional establishment, with low ceilings and low lighting. Its name stems not from a drinking phrase but from the fact that it was very close to the gallows that used to stand in the square: The "last drop" refers to the fall to the end of the rope. Deacon Brodies Tavern (on Lawnmarket) is also a traditional pub. Because of its position in the heart of town, you will find just as many visitors as locals here, with people trading travel stories.

> **If you want to strike up a conversation, the weather is still one of the most popular topics in Scotland.**

SPORTS

Rugby

Edinburgh is the home of Scottish Rugby Union, and the stadium can be found at Murrayfield, west of the city center. Matches are held only intermittently, however The Calcutta Cup Match, in early April, pits the Scots against their "auld" enemy — the English — and is a great spectacle. For tickets and information, contact Murrayfield Stadium (Tel. 346 5000).

Football

Football (soccer) is a passion in Scotland, though the two most successful teams are from Glasgow. Edinburgh has two Premier

A rugby match may offer a bit of excitement to those who like spectator sports. Try to catch a game or two.

Division (the top division) teams: Heart of Midlothian (Hearts), playing at the Tynecastle Park ground on McLeod Street (Tel. 200 7201), and Hibernian (Hibs), who play at the Easter Road Stadium (Tel. 661 1875). Games are scheduled on Wednesdays and Saturdays from September through April.

Athletics

Meadowbank Stadium, in the east of the city, is a premier venue for athletics (track and field). It hosted the Commonwealth Games in 1970 and has a schedule of events throughout the summer.

Walking and Hiking

You can take one of the numerous guided walking tours through the Old and New Towns. Specialty walks — Writers' Edinburgh, Ghostly "Wynds," or a pub tour — enable you to tailor your strolling to your interests (see GUIDES AND TOURS, page 118).

Holyrood Park, within the confines of the city, provides an ideal area for walking. For many visitors, the view of Edinburgh from Arthur's Seat is one of the highlights of a trip to the city. The walk up this volcanic peak is steep but within the capability of a normally fit person. You can set your own pace, though most people manage to reach the top in around an hour. On most days of the year you'll have lots of company — and people to help if you get into difficulty. Take a picnic and enjoy an alfresco lunch at this spectacular spot.

Golf

Edinburgh has a long affiliation with the game. Indeed, it is said that Scotland gave golf to the world. Leith Links is considered the "home of golf," and there are another five municipal courses in the area. The Edinburgh and Lothians Tourist Board offers the "Lothians and Edinburgh Golf Pass," with discounted rates on 20 courses in the Lothians region.

Just 88 km (55 miles) north of Edinburgh is St. Andrews, a hallowed destination for golfers from around the world and one of the premier professional courses on the international tour. It is quite possible to play a round on a day excursion from Edinburgh.

Skiing

To the west of the city at Hillend is Midlothian Ski Centre, the longest artificial ski slope in Europe. Hillend is open year round and has all the equipment you need for rent (Tel. 445 4433).

SHOPPING

Where to Shop

Edinburgh draws the best of Scottish products to its stores and provides a ready marketplace for goods from the northern Highlands and islands. The major shopping street is Princes Street, considered the Oxford Street of Scotland.

Here you'll find — among many major British names — Edinburgh's traditional department store, Jenners, which has been a local institution for generations. The store has a wonderful Art Deco interior to match its ornate exterior. The streets running parallel to Princes Street in the New Town also have shops and boutiques, and there are several antique shops on the Georgian streets north of Queen Street.

The Old Town also has interesting stores to explore and browse. At the top of the Royal Mile you'll see typical tourist paraphernalia (postcards and T-shirts), but in the narrow surrounding streets there are many individual stores selling antiques, books, curios, and collectibles.

If it's raining or cold, Edinburgh has two malls where you can shop in comfort. The Waverley Shopping Centre (where you will also find the Tourist Information Centre) is on Princes Street next to Waverley Street Station, and the larger St. James Centre (with the central post office) is on Leith Street at the eastern end of Princes Street.

Tracing Your Ancestors

In the last few centuries, there have been numerous mass emigrations from Scotland to new lands around the world. Many visitors from the United States, Canada, Australia, New Zealand, and South Africa have Scottish ancestry and want to find out more about their family ties. Help is at hand at the Scottish Genealogy Society and Family History Centre, where nonmembers can take a research session for £5 (15 Victoria Terrace; Tel. 220 3677; open Tuesday 10:30am–5:30pm, Wednesday 10:30am–8:30pm, Thursday 10:30am–5pm, and Saturday 10am–5pm).

If you don't want to attempt the task yourself, a private company that offers a free initial consultation is Scottish Roots Ancestral Service (16 Forth Street; Tel. 477 8214).

What to Buy

Woolens and Woven Goods¶

Tartan. Tartan fabric is synonymous with Scotland, with many items and patterns to choose from. The major Scottish families had their own traditional tartan patterns that instantly identified their clan and kinship. If you have any Scottish ancestry, you will be able to find the tartan for you; otherwise, it is a matter of finding a pattern that you like. All tartan patterns must be registered, and one of the most recent is the new Britannia tartan, commissioned especially for the *Royal Yacht Britannia* in its new Scottish home. You will be able to buy it at the giftshop adjacent to the ship on your visit.

Traditionally tartans were worn in the form of a kilt or traditional Highland dress, and these are certainly still available. Today, however, you can buy almost anything with a tartan pattern: scarves, hats, kitchen aprons, waistcoats (vests), tote bags, teddy bears — the list is almost endless! The Edinburgh Weaving Company (on Castlehill) has over 150 tartans for sale but will also custom make a kilt for you to take home.

Woolens. Scotland is world renowned for its wool and the quality of its finished products. The northern islands produce beautiful, heavy-

Merchants offer a wide array of classic Scotch kilts and tartan fabric.

knitted Fair Isle and Arran sweaters, which are available in stores throughout the city. In more modern times (after the Industrial Revolution), cashmere was introduced to the weavers; the softer garments produced from this wool make good souvenirs or presents. Pack lightly and buy a warm sweater when you arrive in town to keep off the summer chills or winter winds.

Tweed is also produced from wool, manufactured into jackets, coats, and suits. Tweed traditionally kept lairds and lords warm as they went out on grouse shoots on their northern estates — before the invention of Goretex.

Synonymous with golf, Pringle clothing is made in Edinburgh at its manufacturing base at 70–74 Bangor Road, Leith (Tel. 553 5161). You can visit the factory throughout the year or buy from stores in the city center. The fine weave and pattern are typical of a Scottish weaver's attention to detail.

Glassware and Pottery

Traditional skills extend wider than weaving. High-quality pottery and glassware are also produced here. Edinburgh Crystal, at Penicuik (a twenty-minute ride from the city center), produces a beautiful range of cut glassware in the form of glasses, decanters, and bowls. Other producers in Scotland are Stuart Crystal and Caithness Glass, both of which have beautiful patterns and a wide range of goods.

Bagpipes

The mournful lament of the single pipe is a sound that is always associated with Scotland, and you will certainly hear it as you travel around the city. You will find Scottish pipes still being handmade in the heart of the city. Kilberry Bagpipes (at Gilmore Place, Tollcross) manufactures and sells traditional, professional instruments in a range of sizes.

Books

Edinburgh has been at the forefront of publishing and printing for centuries. It supported the work of the university, which was a major center of learning from the 16th century, particularly in law, medicine, and veterinary practice. Although publishing itself has declined in importance, one legacy of the industry is the number of bookstores selling second-hand, antiquarian, and new books. The Edinburgh-based James Thin has the largest bookstore in Scotland (on George Street, opposite the university buildings of Chambers Street).

You might not find the signed first edition of your dreams. But with the wealth of writing talent that has graced the city, books by Burns, Scott, and Stevenson (along with poetry by Ramsey) make very suitable souvenirs of your trip.

Antiques and Clocks

As a capital city, Edinburgh has its own office for the stamping of gold and silver, with the city's mark found on many antique pieces. If you find an old "tappit hen" (a traditional drinking tankard), look for the silver assay mark of a castle, indicating an authentic Edinburgh piece.

Clockmaking has been a strong tradition since the 1500s. A good piece commands a high price.

The finest in crystal glassware is available in the nearby town of Penicuik.

Jewelry, Silver, and Other Crafts

From the days of the Stuart kings, Scottish jewelry was known for the high quality of its workmanship. Use of traditional Scottish materials such as silver — and stones such as carnelian or agate — make for unique pieces. Often local Celtic patterns appear in bracelets, brooches (pins), and scarf rings.

Arts and crafts are held in high regard in Edinburgh. Beautiful examples of enamelware, ceramics, and pottery are produced in great abundance, often following a Celtic theme.

Food and Drink

Edinburgh produces a range of edible (and drinkable) souvenirs that can make great presents for folks back home.

Edinburgh rock. A confection found only here, Edinburgh rock is a sugar, water, and coloring mixture that is boiled and then cooled on stone slabs before being shaped. The "rock" has a soft texture and can be bought in a variety of shapes.

Haggis. This nutritious and tasty dish is at the heart of Scottish cuisine, and you'll be able to buy it in all sizes to take home. For those who find the traditional sheep's stomach casing a little off-putting, haggis is now produced in a range of outer casings, including heat-resistant plastic.

Shortbread and oatcakes. Oatmeal was a staple ingredient of Scottish cuisine from the very earliest days and is now available in the form of oatcakes. For those who prefer something sweeter, shortbread (traditionally served at Yuletide and Hogmanay) is rich in butter and sugar. You will find pretty tins of both types of biscuits for sale in the city, often decorated with city or highland scenes.

Salmon and kippers. The kippers you enjoy for breakfast or the smoked salmon served as an evening appetizer can be bought prepacked for your journey home.

Whisky. It is said that the Scots invented whisky, and the national drink is now one of Scotland's major exports. The subtle blend of pure spring water, malt, and yeast — aged in oak barrels — is unique to each distillery of single malt whisky. The diverse range of flavors makes exploration of single malts a fascinating one. Try a selection at the Whisky Heritage Centre (they have over 100 for you to sample), where you can then buy a bottle or two of your personal favorite in the shop or in stores around the city.

Drambuie. Since receiving Bonnie Prince Charlie's recipe in the 18th century, the MacKinnon family still owns the secret recipe for this alcoholic beverage.

Glavya. Glavya is a blend of whisky, herbal oils, honey, and sugar.

ACTIVITIES FOR CHILDREN

Edinburgh has a wealth of activities for children to enjoy. Take them to Edinburgh Castle for stories of heroism and great views of the city. Stay to hear the One O'Clock Gun — but note that it is very loud, so prepare little ones for the surprise! Nearby, the Lookout Tower and Camera Obscura offer a unique view of the city. Just be prepared for several fights of stairs to reach the top of the building.

Explore the story of our planet at Our Dynamic Earth. Here you can experience an earthquake, touch an iceberg, and listen to the sound of a rain forest all in one place.

The colorful carousel in Princes Street Gardens is fun for the young at heart.

Edinburgh Zoo has a penguin parade every day during the summer. You can't help falling in love with these creatures, who march along in their black and white "uniforms."

In May every year, the Scottish International Children's Festival holds arts, theater, and dance activities and performances especially for children aged 8 to 15. During the summer festival season, children will be fascinated by the street theater, clowns, face painting, and temporary tattooing.

If your children are tired of trudging city streets, take a ride to Portobello (on the Firth of Forth), where the long sandy beach offers a perfect environment for long walks, kite flying, or wading and swimming in the sea.

Treat your little "ladies and gentlemen" to high tea. They are sure to rise to the occasion of cucumber sandwiches, cakes, and scones served on fine bone china.

Calendar of Events

25 January Burns Night celebrations mark the birthday of poet Robert Burns.

early April Calcutta Cup, the annual rugby union match between Scotland and England.

end of May Scottish International Children's Festival.

June Royal Highland Show.

July and August Edinburgh International Jazz and Blues Festival.

August Edinburgh Military Tattoo (first to last week in month).
Edinburgh International Festival (mid-August to early September)
Edinburgh Festival Fringe (last three weeks of month)
Edinburgh International Film Festival (second half of month)
Edinburgh International Book Festival (second half of month)

31 December Hogmanay, arguably the most authentic New Year celebration in the world.

EATING OUT

The Scots are proud of a cuisine distinct from that of the English, and they have contributed many fine ingredients to the British national palate of cooking styles. The clean air, pure water, and acres of open lowlands and hills offer a range of quality produce: from wild game and other meats to fish, seafood, vegetables, and fruit. Modern Scottish cooking uses the best of these ingredients, and there are several "native" restaurants in the city with an international reputation for serving the best in quality and variety.

However, Edinburgh is not just a city of Scottish cuisine. It has restaurants ranging from Indonesian to Thai to Mexican. The city's population of urbane lawyers, academics, doctors, and artists demands the best, and the quality of eateries in the city is generally very high. As Edinburgh takes its place as the parliamentary capital of Scotland, its new profile is attracting interest and investment from the biggest names in the culinary world, ensuring a vibrant era of new and exciting eateries.

The Edinburgh and Lothians Tourist Board produces the *Edinburgh Food Guide,* which is available from tourist information offices. The *Taste of Scotland* brochure highlights a number of restaurants serving traditional Scottish food.

When to Eat

Breakfast is usually served in hotels between 7:30am and 10am. Because most hotels include it in the price of your room, you will find few places in town offering breakfast.

In restaurants lunch is from noon to 2:30pm, though many pubs will serve food all day. Set business lunches are a good deal, and many restaurants in the city offer them Monday through Friday. You will also find numerous sandwich bars and cafés for a quick snack. There are good cafés in Edinburgh Castle, the Scottish Museum, and Our Dynamic Earth for snacks and lunch dishes.

High tea is rather more than an afternoon snack; it is generally served between 3pm and 5pm.

Dinner is normally served from 6:30pm to 10:30pm, but many establishments serve later on weekends and during the summer season. Many restaurants, including some of the most renowned, will offer pre- or post-theater special menus, serving early or late depending on your needs. These are very popular — especially during the festival season — so you should book tables in advance.

What To Eat

Historically, the highland farmers and clansmen had meager diets. The land and the rivers belonged to powerful landowners, and taking wild or managed livestock or fish from the rivers was considered poaching. If you were caught, the severe punishments included deportation or even death.

In poorer households, oatmeal formed a major part of the diet, and there were mills in every settlement to grind the meal. Porridge (oatmeal cooked with water and salt) was eaten for breakfast, and oatcakes were served at every meal, supplemented by vegetables and a little protein. Oatmeal is still a popular ingredient in many Scottish dishes, where it is used to add fiber and texture. But today's visitors can also sample meats and seafood from the land in a range of native dishes.

Breakfast

Breakfast can be a feast, even in the smallest B&Bs. It can prepare you for the rest of the day, and it might even see those on a budget through until dinner.

A full Scottish breakfast will always include bacon, sausage, black pudding (blood sausage), eggs, tomatoes, mushrooms, and toast. Many hotels will also offer juice and cereal as part of the full breakfast package. If this is a little too much to eat first thing in the morning, lighter traditional breakfasts include *smoked kippers* (herring) from Loch Fyne or *finan haddie* (fillet of haddock smoked with peat) poached in milk.

Another nutritious start to the day is *kedgeree,* consisting of a delicious mixture of flaked fish, rice, and hard-boiled eggs. The local Scottish fish add an extra special taste to the finished dish.

Porridge might sound like a light option, but a bowl full of oatmeal cooked with milk is actually very filling. Cool it by pouring more milk over it and add salt to taste — or sugar, though the Scots scoff at sweetening it.

Scotland also produces the most delicious jams and honey, particularly from the wild fruits and heather of the northern highlands. These can be enjoyed on toast or added to porridge.

Soups and Broths

Soups and thick broths have always been popular in Scotland, particularly in winter. Cooks often made a few ingredients go a long way, especially in poorer crofter families in the countryside. The internationally known *Scotch broth* comprises vegetable soup made with mutton stock and thickened with barley and lentils; *cock-a-leekie* is a soup of chicken and leeks. *Bawd bree* (hare soup) is seen less often on menus. You'll also find seafood soups: *Cullen skink* is a combination of smoked haddock, onions, potatoes and milk; *partan bree* is cream of crab meat.

> **When ordering food in a pub, you will need to go to the bar. There is no table service.**

A hearty Scottish breakfast is not for the light eater. Oatmeal is followed by eggs, bacon, black pudding, and more!

Main Dishes

The Scottish countryside offers an abundance of quality fresh ingredients for the table. The woods and moors still have healthy hunting and shooting industries. Partridge, grouse, pheasant, and venison all form the basis of very tasty meals. The domesticated livestock industry is also extremely good, with beef from Aberdeen Angus cattle considered among the best in the world. You can find it readily on menus in the city. The local lamb is also excellent.

Simple broiled or roasted meat is standard, but you can also find it accompanied by sauce (perhaps red wine) or served slow-cooked in a stew with onions and seasonal vegetables.

Haggis is perhaps the most famous Scottish dish. It was originally a poor man's dish, made from parts of the animal left after the major cuts had been taken. Very little of the animal was wasted in centuries past, and haggis developed as a method of making a little meat — and not the prettiest parts — taste good and feed a lot of people. Haggis is traditionally made with the "pluck" of a sheep (the windpipe, lungs, heart, and liver). The windpipe is removed and the other parts are boiled for three hours. The fat is skimmed off and the parts are minced. Oatmeal, onion, seasoning, spices, and gravy are then added, and the entire mixture is stuffed into a sheep's "paunch" or stomach (modern haggis may be encased in an artificial skin.) The stuffed skin is then simmered in water for one to two hours.

A haggis must always be served as hot as possible. To serve, cut the haggis lengthwise and scoop out the meat mixture. The casing is discarded, and only the filling is put on the plate. It is traditionally eaten with *bashed neeps* (mashed turnip) and *tatties* (mashed potatoes).

Fish and seafood are also popular, although catches from the nearby seas and rivers have been diminishing. Salmon was, until recently, a fish available only to rich landowners, caught in their private rivers. Smoked sea fish such as haddock or herring were traditionally on a working-class menu, produced in smoking sheds along the coast of the Firth of Forth before being transported the short way to the residential areas of the city.

Today, class lines have been blurred, and the most modest of fish dishes have become fashionable. River salmon and trout remain expensive, but the supply has been supplemented in recent years by farmed fish (although aficionados will argue that the taste is not the same as wild fish).

Smoked salmon can be enjoyed as an appetizer with bread and butter, or the whole fish might be poached as an entrée. You will also find *finan haddie* or *Arbroath smokies* (also haddock, smoked with oak chips) — so if you can't face fish for breakfast, you can enjoy it for dinner.

You will find fish of many non-Scottish varieties, but the traditional local method of preparation is to sauté them with a crisp oatmeal coating.

Desserts

The Scots are known for their sweet tooth. Wild fruits from the land — raspberries, blackberries, rhubarb, and gooseberries, among others — formed the basis of many pies and puddings, often with a crisp coating of oatmeal. *Cranachan* is a dish of raspberries and cream topped with toasted oatmeal. *Atholl brose* is a delicious blend of whisky, honey, cream, and oatmeal — a rather adult version of porridge. *Auld alliance* creamed cheese laced with whisky is traditionally eaten as a spread on toasted bread.

Cheese can also be found in great variety, served once again with oatmeal in the form of oatcakes, allowing the natural flavor of the cheese to come through. Try Dunlop, not unlike cheddar; Lanark Blue, a Roquefort-style blue cheese; or Bonchester, a Camembert-style offering.

Shortbread was originally an oatmeal bread served at Yuletide, though it was a food carried over from pagan times. Made in a circle and pinched around the edge with the finger, it was meant to symbolize the rays of the sun that would bring rebirth to the land in spring. The oatmeal was subsequently replaced by finer milled flour to create the shortbread biscuit we eat today. Rich in sugar and butter, it goes well with tea and coffee and is often served at the end of a meal.

High Tea

The prim ladies for whom Edinburgh is famed — in the style of Miss Jean Brodie — would shop in town and take tea at one of the fine hotels or cafés as a finale to their afternoon. This tradition continues, a perfect activity for visitors to sit and relax in a genteel environment after a day of sightseeing (between 3pm and 5pm). In addition to small sandwiches and cream cakes, you might find such uniquely Scottish delights as potato scones, *Dundee cake* (a rich fruitcake decorated with almonds), or *black bun* (a cake flavored with dried fruit ginger mixed with cinnamon and brandy). Jams and honey made with produce from the countryside are a delicious accompaniment.

WHAT TO DRINK

Whisky

Without doubt, the king of Scottish drinks is whisky, a concoction that the Scots are said to have invented. (Don't say this in a bar in Ireland. The two populations have been in friendly dispute about the origin of whisky for generations.) *Whisky* is a Gaelic word derived from the phrase *uisge beatha,* meaning "water of life." It is a blend of pure spring water, malted barley or grain, and yeast, which is distilled and then aged in oak barrels. But this simple recipe belies the richness and variety of the finished product.

Two factors are important for the flavor of the finished product. The first is the

Street kiosks near Princes Street Gardens provide a variety of delicious snacks.

water from which the whisky is made, imparting the particular taste of each brand. Scottish water is considered particularly good for the production of a distilled alcohol, but it tastes different in different parts of the country (some waters are filtered through peat, imparting a particular flavor to the finished drink). The second factor is the shape of the still used in the distillation process. Each shape produces a different finished alcohol, the clear spirit that is then aged in oak casks.

The nearest working distillery to the city, Glenkinchie, produces a very soft lowland malt that is said to be a perfect introduction to single malts for the beginner. You will find that most bars and hotels will have a range of malts and blended whiskies for you to try. The Heritage Whisky Centre has well over 100 from all parts of Scotland, and you can get information about the particular attributes of each drink.

Single malts. Whiskies produced from malted barley and bottled direct from the barrel are called "single malts," and each of the over 100 produced by different distilleries in Scotland is distinctive in its taste. This diverse range of flavors makes exploring and sampling single malts a fascinating pursuit. Lowland malts (from the area in the south of Scotland) are softer in style and flavor; Speyside malts (from farther north, west of Inverness) are considered the "cream" of single malt; Highland and island malts (Isla, Arran, Jura, Sky, Mull) are unique in their flavor, often heavy with heather peat, producing a taste that has been described as "medicinal."

> Whisky is generally served neat, with ice, or with a little water. If you drink it with club soda, you might get a friendly lecture from a Scotsman.

Malt whisky is aged for a number of years in oak barrels before being bottled; the minimum time is three years, but some are aged for 15 or 20. Aging refines the taste and imparts the distinctive color to the whisky. Some distilleries use barrels imported from Spain, originally used to age sherry and giving a slight sweetness to the finished whisky.

Blended whisky. In the past both the quality and quantity of whisky production would vary, and the flavor of many single malts was not suited to the taste of the mass population. In the 18th century, a group of distillers decided to create a standard product that could be produced in batches for consistency and palatability. They began to produce whisky from grains other than malted barley and to mix different whiskies (malts and nonmalts) together, producing

The gaelic name for whisky, "uisge beatha," translates to "water of life."

the blended whiskies of today. Blends contain whiskies of different ages — up to 40 different whiskies in one blend. When a blend has an age on the label, it is the age of the youngest whisky in the blend.

The art of whisky blenders is a fine one. They smell different aged whiskies to create a blend, very much as a perfumier creates a fragrance. Only a few individuals have the "nose" for the job, and this has often been a hereditary occupation, passed from father to son.

Drambuie

Drambuie was said to be Bonnie Prince Charlie's favorite drink. He bequeathed its secret recipe to his friend MacKinnon of Straithard in gratitude for organizing the prince's escape from the English army in 1745. The drink was made in small quantities for family consumption until 1906, when it went on general sale. The MacKinnon family still owns the company and has continued to keep the recipe for drambuie a secret while making a success of the commercial production. Interestingly, the recipe has been passed down through the female line of the family.

Glavya

First produced in 1940, *glavya* (meaning "very good") is a blend of whisky, herbal oils, honey, and sugar. Ronald Morrison and George Petrie, a chemist, worked together at their Leith blending works to perfect the taste. To preserve its secrecy, the recipe for glavya is known by only three people at any one time.

Beer

Edinburgh has several working breweries, and the faint smell of warm hops often blows across the city on the prevailing breeze. Caledonian Brewery is probably the largest, producing various types of beer that are on sale in pubs throughout the city. It has won many accolades for its brews in recent years and concentrates on traditional methods of production.

Its most famed beer is 80/- ("Eighty Shilling") named after the cost of the excise duty on a consignment in times past. Stronger beer had more excise duty, weaker beer less. So for many years if you ordered a Caledonian beer in a bar, you asked for a 60/-, 80/-, or 120/- in order of increasing strength. Other Caledonian beers include Deuchars IPA, Burns Ale. and Golden Promise, an organic beer.

HANDY TRAVEL TIPS

An A–Z Summary of Practical Information

A

ACCOMMODATIONS

Edinburgh offers an extensive range of accommodations: luxury hotels, historic houses, more modest hotels, boarding houses, simple bed-and-breakfast establishments, and backpackers' hostels.

Hotels and guesthouses that have been inspected and approved by the Scottish Tourist Board (STB) are given ratings according to the number and type of facilities (from one to five crowns) and also according to standards of service ("Approved," "Commended," or "Highly Commended"). The STB makes its assessments through personal visits and updates its information annually. This includes full details of prices and facilities (see TOURIST INFORMATION page 128).

In the high season (July–September), and especially during the three weeks of the Edinburgh International Festival, the city becomes particularly crowded and rooms are at a premium. Should you intend to visit during this period, you are strongly advised to book accommodations as far in advance as possible.

However, if you do find yourself in Edinburgh without a hotel reservation, head for one of the city's Tourist Information and Accommodation Centres (on Princes Street or at Edinburgh International Airport), where the staff will try to find a room for you.

The Edinburgh and Lothians Tourist Office produces a number of brochures. Most helpful is *Where to Stay and What to Do,* listing accommodations in all categories (including campsites) as well as attractions in the area. There is also a winter *Short Breaks* brochure for special accommodation offers between October and March each year.

In publicity materials, prices for rooms are almost always quoted as "per person per night." Breakfast is usually included, but do check before making a reservation. Rooms in most hotels have private bathrooms, but some B&Bs (particularly at the budget end of the market) will have shared facilities. Always make sure you know what is included in the price of the room. VAT is always included in the price, but service charges (between 10% and 15%) might not be.

For those on a budget who do not want to stay in a backpackers' hostel, all three Edinburgh universities offer accommodations in their halls of residence. This is cheaper than most hotels but not always cheaper than a B&B in a private house. However, you can be assured that the Scottish Tourist Board has assessed the quality of the university rooms, which is not always the case with private B&Bs. Edinburgh First, at the University of Edinburgh, is the most central (Tel. toll-free 0800 128 7118 within the UK only, otherwise Tel. 651 2044; fax 667-7271; e-mail: <jeanette.wells@ed.ac.uk>).

AIRPORTS

Edinburgh International Airport (Tel. 333 1000) lies 12 km (8 miles) west of the city. There are no direct international flights from outside Europe, but you can get many connections from London, Brussels, Amsterdam, Frankfurt, Dublin, and other European hubs. Bus services link the airport with the city (Waverley Station) every 15-minutes during the day at a cost of £3 one way. Taxi fare is £13, with travel time around 20-minutes.

Glasgow International Airport is a one-hour drive from Edinburgh, with direct flights from North America (daily connections from New York, Toronto, and Chicago). Onward travel to Edinburgh can be undertaken by bus (1 hr 45 minutes), with one-way fares of £8. There is also a rail service from Glasgow's city center to Edinburgh's Waverley Station (50 minutes), with one-way fares of £7.

BICYCLE RENTAL

Edinburgh takes care of its cyclists, offering bicycle paths and allowing cyclists to use separate bus lanes in the city center. Cyclists can also take advantage of the narrow alleyways of the Old Town, where cars cannot travel. Because the center of Edinburgh has many hills and inclines, cycling here requires a certain level of fitness.

A map of cycle routes (£3) is available from the Edinburgh and Lothians Tourist Office to help you make the most of your trip. Edinburgh Cycle Hire rents bicycles (29 Blackfriars Street, Tel. 556 5560).

BUDGETING FOR YOUR TRIP

Britain is a relatively expensive place to visit, especially for visitors from North America, Australia, and New Zealand. Here are a few guidelines to help you plan your budget.

Accommodations: £50–£60 per person per night for a medium room.

Meals: dinner £25-£40 per person in a moderate restaurant, without drinks. Most accommodations include breakfast in the price, and a full Scottish breakfast will really set you up for the day.

Domestic airfare: about £140 (roundtrip/return) from London Heathrow to Edinburgh.

Car rental: £200 per week for a small vehicle.

Bus travel: £2.50 day pass; 70p single trip.

Museums and galleries: £6.50 for adults to enter Edinburgh Castle; many other city museums and galleries are free.

Theatre tickets: £20–£30 for a mid-price ticket.

Walking tour of the Old Town: £5–£10.

Bus tour of the city: £8–£13.

CAMPING

The Edinburgh and Lothians Tourist brochure *Where to Stay and What to Do* describes all campgrounds and caravan (trailer) parks. Most of these sit along the coast or are a short drive from the city center in the Scottish countryside, making them the perfect base for a city–country vacation.

CAR RENTAL

If you plan to spend your time in Edinburgh city center, a vehicle will probably be more of a hindrance than a help. The city is compact, which is great for strolling, and parking in the city is difficult. However, if you plan to take trips into the surrounding countryside, you will want to rent a car.

Car rentals in Britain are relatively expensive by international standards, but the condition of the vehicles (mostly new) and the customer support are excellent. All the major car-rental companies — Hertz, Avis, and Europcar — have desks at Edinburgh's airport, and it is possible to pick up a car immediately upon your arrival in the city. If you arrive by train, you can arrange to pick up a car in the city.

Some of the larger rental companies offer more competitive rates if you reserve the car from home rather than when you arrive in the UK. It pays, therefore, to sketch out your itinerary before departing for the UK so that you can make a reservation and plan pick-up and drop-off points.

A small car will cost around £200 per week, medium-sized cars around £270; all companies add approximately £50 per week for a car with automatic transmission. Insurance covers collision damage and theft, but personal accident insurance runs an extra £3 or £4 per day. Many companies have a minimum age (usually 21) for drivers. Credit cards are the preferred method of payment, and you will need to show your license when you pick up the car.

CLIMATE

Southern Scotland has a temperate climate influenced by its proximity to the Atlantic Ocean. It is characterized by warm, wet summers and cold, wet winters. Even in summer, cold spells can occur and the weather can change quickly. Average monthly temperatures (which can and do vary) are as follows:

	J	F	M	A	M	J	J	A	S	O	N	D
°C	4	5	7	10	14	17	19	18	15	11	7	6
°F	39	41	44	50	58	62	66	64	59	52	44	43

Edinburgh

CLOTHING

With Edinburgh's often chilly climate, a trip requires several different types of clothing even if you travel in summer. A layering system is the best approach so that you can take off or add clothing as necessary. A rainproof outer layer is a must whatever time of year you travel, along with an umbrella. In winter, a thick coat or jacket, gloves, and a hat will keep you warm in cold spells, when the wind can bite.

On warm summer days, T-shirts, light shirts, and slacks or light dresses make ideal clothing. But always carry an extra layer just in case, and take a light sweater or jacket for the evenings. Comfortable shoes are a must for the daytime.

In the evenings, casual attire is acceptable in most restaurants. If you intend to eat at some of the finer restaurants or visit the ballet or theatre, a shirt and tie for men and "dressy" ensemble for women might be appropriate.

COMPLAINTS

Complaints should be taken up first with the establishment concerned. If you are still dissatisfied, then approach the Edinburgh and Lothians Tourist Board. They should be able to direct you to the appropriate body to further advice.

CRIME AND SAFETY

The center of Edinburgh is fairly safe compared to other large European cities. All the same, you should take the usual precautions against theft: Don't carry large amounts of cash, leave your valuables in the hotel safe (not in your room), and beware of pickpockets in crowded areas. Never leave your bags or valuables on view in a parked car — take them with you or lock them in the trunk. Any theft or loss must be reported immediately to the police in order to comply with your travel insurance. If your passport is lost or stolen, you should also inform your consulate.

You will find that the city streets are relatively busy, since Edinburgh is still a residential city and people walk to and from their social engagements far more than in many other British cities. This makes walking safe, but always make sure that you walk in well-lit streets rather than secluded alleyways late at night.

CUSTOMS AND ENTRY REQUIREMENTS

Citizens of the US, Canada, Ireland, Australia, and New Zealand need only a valid passport to enter the UK for a holiday. Citizens of South Africa are required to show a valid passport and a return ticket. All passports must be valid for six months beyond the intended length of stay in the UK.

There are no currency restrictions when entering or leaving the UK, for either British or foreign currencies.

Upon arrival you will have to complete an entry card stating the address where you will be staying. The immigration officer will stamp your passport, allowing you to stay in Britain for a specific length of time. If your plans are uncertain, ask for several months so you don't have to apply for an extension later. Provided you look respectable and have sufficient funds to cover your stay, there should not be a problem.

Visitors may enter the UK with any goods intended for personal use. Visitors arriving from non-EU countries are allowed to bring the following into the UK duty free: 200 cigarettes or 50 cigars or 250 grams of tobacco; 1 liter of beverages with over 22% alcohol or 2 liters for beverages with less than 22% alcohol or 2 liters of fortified or sparkling wine; 2 liters of wine; 50 grams of perfume or 250 ml of toilet water; and other goods to the value of £136.

In British ports and airports, passengers with goods to declare follow the red channel; those with nothing to declare take the green route.

D

DRIVING

If you are bringing your own car or one from Europe, you will need the registration papers and insurance coverage. The usual formula is the Green Card, an extension to existing insurance that validates it for other countries. Don't forget your driver's license.

Rules and regulations. Remember to drive on the left. Pay special attention at corners (crossings) and traffic circles (roundabouts). Traffic that is already in the circle has the right of way over cars waiting to enter the circle, and the rule is to give way to the right.

Drivers and front-seat passengers must use seat belts; rear-seat passengers must also use seat belts if they are present. Motorcycle riders must wear a crash helmet, and a driver's license is required for all types of motorcycle. Sixteen is the minimum age for mopeds, seventeen for motorcycles and scooters.

In built-up urban areas, the speed limit is 30 or 40 mph (48 or 64 km/hr); on expressways 70 mph (112 km/hr); and on most other roads and two-lane highways 50 or 60 mph (80 or 96 km/hr). The prevailing speed limit is posted on round signs at the side of the road.

Edinburgh has a number of special lanes for buses and taxis only. These usually operate 7:30am–9:30am and 4:30pm–6:30pm, easing the traffic flow at peak times. You will also find one-way streets that help prevent bottlenecks. If you intend to drive around the city, it would help to invest in a good map to aid navigation.

Road conditions. There are three main types of roads: motorways (expressways), A roads (trunk roads that link all the major towns) and B roads (rural roads). Driving conditions in the UK are generally very good, and all A roads are of good quality.

Fuel costs. Gasoline (petrol) is expensive in the UK: approximately 80p per liter. Most garages have self-service pumps, all of which give measurements in liters. You will find stations in all major towns. The normal hours of operation for fuel are 9am–5:30pm, but this can vary enormously. Hours are extended in the summer months.

Parking. You can park at the side of the street provided there are no restrictions. Many streets will have sections for resident parking with fines for those who break the rules. Street parking is expensive, with costs of over £1.50/hr. Both street parking and parking lots throughout the city operate on a "Pay and Display" system — you purchase a ticket from a machine and display the ticket on your dashboard.

For assistance. Most rental cars come with coverage from a reputable recovery or breakdown service. The Automobile Association (AA), the Royal Automobile Club (RAC), and Green Flag are the most well known; telephone numbers and other contact information are included with your rental documents.

Road signs. Britain has adopted the same basic system of pictographs in use throughout Europe. The *Highway Code* is the official booklet of road usage and signs, available at most bookshops. We provide "translations" for the following written signs found throughout Britain:

British	**American**
Carriageway	*Roadway*
Clearway	*No parking by highway*
Diversion	*Detour*
Dual carriageway	*Divided highway*
Give way	*Yield*
Level crossing	*Railroad crossing*
Motorway	*Expressway, freeway*
No overtaking	*No passing*
Roadworks	*Men working*
Roundabout	*Traffic circle*

Fluid measures

115

Distance

km	0	1	2	3	4	5	6	8	10	12	14	16
miles	0	½	1	1½	2	3	4	5	6	7	8	9	10

E

ELECTRICITY

The standard current in England is 240 volt, 50 cycle AC. All visitors (except South Africans) will need an adapter (with square 3-pin plugs) for any appliance brought from home, as well as a converter unless the appliance is equipped with one. Adapters are available at airport shops. Most hotels have special sockets for shavers and hairdryers that operate on 240 or 110 volts.

EMBASSIES, CONSULATES, AND HIGH COMMISSIONS

Many countries have consuls or other representatives in Edinburgh, but others have representation only in London.

Australia: Australian High Commission, 23 Mitchell Street, Edinburgh EH6 7BD; Tel. 467 8333.

Canada: Canadian Consulate, Standard Life House, 30 Lothian Road, Edinburgh EH2 2XZ; Tel. 220 4333.

Ireland: Consulate General of Ireland, 16 Randolph Crescent, Edinburgh EH3 7TT; Tel. 226 7711.

New Zealand: New Zealand High Commission, New Zealand House, 80 Haymarket, London SW1Y 4TQ; Tel. 0171 930 8422.

South Africa: South African Embassy, South Africa House, Trafalgar Square, London WC2N 5DP; Tel. 0171 930 4488.

US: American Consulate General, 3 Regent Terrace, Edinburgh EH7 5BW; Tel. 556 8315.

EMERGENCIES

The emergency telephone number is the same throughout the United Kingdom. Dial **999** and you will be connected to an operator who will ask you the nature of the emergency. The operator will then be able to summon police, firefighters, ambulance (medical aid),or all three services depending on the nature of the emergency. It would be helpful to have as many details as possible about your location when you phone the emergency services.

G

GAY AND LESBIAN TRAVELERS

Edinburgh has a lively gay scene, and there are several gay pubs and discos in the city center. The Gay and Lesbian Centre (58a–60 Broughton Street) is the place to obtain more information. There is a monthly magazine called *Scotsgay,* which also has a website <www.scotsgay.co.uk>. The Lothian Gay and Lesbian Switchboard can provide information on virtually any topic of interest (nightly 7:30pm–10pm, Tel. 556 4049; e-mail: <lgls@itek-uk.com>; website: <www.lgls.org>). *The List,* which is the club, theater, and cinema guide for Edinburgh and Glasgow, also lists venues of particular interest to the gay community.

GETTING THERE

By air. Although Edinburgh Airport has no direct flights from outside Europe, connecting flights can be arranged from London's Heathrow and Gatwick airports, Dublin, Amsterdam Schiphol, Brussels, and Frankfurt, among many other British and continental gateways. British Airways, KLM, and their partner companies manage many of these connecting flights. The flight from Heathrow is 1 hour 40 minutes and from Schiphol approximately 2 hours.

Glasgow International Airport is a one-hour drive west of Edinburgh; there are also bus and train services from Glasgow's airport to Edinburgh's city center. You can find direct flights from North America to Glasgow via New York, Toronto, and Chicago.

Edinburgh

By rail. From central London and the London airports there are rail links (through King's Cross Station) to Edinburgh's Waverley Station run by Great North Eastern Railways. The journey takes about 4.5 hours. Contact National Rail Inquiries (within the UK only: Tel. 0345 484950); website: <www.scotrail.co.uk> or <www.raileurope.com> for details of this and other British and European train travel.

By car. Edinburgh is in the north of the UK, reached from England either directly via the A1 (in the east) or via the M6 (in the west); the M6 connects with the M74 and then the A702 to reach Edinburgh. The driving time is approximately 7 hours on either route, depending on traffic and weather conditions.

From Ireland, the Irish Sea Ferry crosses Dun Laoghaire (pronounced "Dun Leary") to Holyhead, Wales; from there, take the M6 for the onward drive to Edinburgh. From mainland Europe, the daily P&O/North Sea Ferry Services (from Rotterdam and Zeebrugge to Hull) link with the A1 via the M62.

By bus. National Express offers a comprehensive network of coach/bus services throughout the UK, with regular service from London's Victoria Station to Edinburgh. You can connect as well via other cities and towns as part of an itinerary. Further details and timetables are available by phone in the UK only (Tel. 0990 505050).

GUIDES AND TOURS

There are several types of tours in the Edinburgh region. Themed walking tours are a great favorite. Some of the options available include the following:

Auld Reekie Tours (45 Niddry Street; Tel. 557 4700; e-mail: <auldreekietour@cablenet.co.uk>) and **Mercat Walking Tours** (City Chambers; Tel./fax 225 6591; website: <www.mercat-tours.co.uk>) both let you travel back in time through narrow alleyways of the Old Town or follow numerous pub, literary, and ghost walks.

Geowalks (23 Summerfield Place; Tel. 555 5488; fax 055 8383; e-mail: <angus@geowalks.demon.co.uk>) features walks around Arthur's Seat, with geological and natural history commentary.

McEwan's 80-Shilling Edinburgh Literary Pub Tour (97b West Bow, Edinburgh EH1 2JP; Tel. 226 6665; fax 226 6668; website: <www.scot-lit-tour.co.uk>), a tour through the old town with commentary by costumed actors depicting literary characters who bring the history to life.

There are also bus and coach tours to attractions in the city, the surrounding Lothians area, and even farther north into Scotland. Pick-up points for these are along Waverley Street outside the railway station. Bus tours to outlying areas such as Lowlands, Highlands, and St. Andrews are also available. One company operating a range of options is Rabbie's Trail Burners (207 High Street, Edinburgh EH1 1PE; Tel. 226 3133; fax 225 7028; website: <www.rabbies.com>). Trips start from £15.

H

HEALTH AND MEDICAL CARE

No vaccinations are needed for a visit to the UK. Tap water is safe to drink. The National Health Service offers free emergency treatment or first aid to all visitors. Free treatment does not apply to dentistry or to consulting an optician. However, for treatment of a more complicated nature or a pre-existing condition, charges will be made. It is always sensible to take out comprehensive medical insurance for your trip.

The main accident and emergency hospital is Edinburgh Royal Infirmary, very close to the Museum of Scotland, on Lauriston Place.

A range of "over-the-counter" drugs is available for everyday ailments. A qualified pharmacist (chemist) will offer advice about the medication you need. There is a late-night dispensing pharmacy at Boots the Chemist (48 Shandwick Place, Edinburgh; Tel. 225 6757).

For emergency dental problems, contact Edinburgh Dental Hospital (Tel. 536 4900).

Edinburgh

HITCHIKING

Hitchhiking is not illegal in Britain. Walking with thumb raised out toward the road is the normal sign that you are looking for a lift. All usual safety warnings apply, and females traveling alone might be vulnerable.

HOLIDAYS

The following dates are public holidays in the city (generally known as "bank holidays" in the UK). This means that offices and banks will be closed, but shops and restaurants remain open. When a bank holiday falls on a Saturday or Sunday, the following Monday will be taken as the official holiday.

1–2 January

Good Friday

Easter Monday

first Monday in May

last Monday in May

last Monday in August

25–26 December (Christmas Day and Boxing Day)

LANGUAGE

English in Edinburgh is spoken with a soft Scottish accent, which can make phrases a little hard to understand. In addition, there is a particular vocabulary which is particular only to this part of Scotland. Gaelic and old Scots words and phrases will baffle the most fluent English speaker. Today just over 82,000 Scots speak Gaelic, most of them living in the Western Isles. However, many place names throughout the country are derived from Gaelic names, and words and phrases from the old Scots dialect (called "Lallans") are still in common use. Here are some examples to help you along:

Scottish/Gaelic	English
auld lang syne	days long ago
Auld Reekie	Edinburgh ("Old Smoky")
aye	yes
bairn	child
ben	mountain
bide a wee	wait a bit
biggin	building
bonny/bonnie	pretty
brae	hillside
bramble	blackberry
brig	bridge
burn	stream
cairn	pile of stones
ceilidh	song and story gathering
clachan	hamlet
croft	small land-holding
dinna fash yersel'	don't get upset
dram	measure of whisky
firth	estuary
ghillie	attendant for hunting or fishing
glen	valley
haud yer wheesht	shut up
Hogmanay	New Year's Eve
inver	mouth of river

Edinburgh

ken	know
kirk	church
knock	knoll
kyle	strait
lang may yer lum reek	long may your chimney smoke (i.e., "may you have a long life")
lassie	girl
links	seaside golfcourse
linn	waterfall
loch	lake
mickle	small amount (*many a mickle maks a muckle* means "little things add up to big things")
mull	promontory
provost	mayor
sett	tartan pattern
skirl	sound of bagpipes
strath	river valley
thunderplump	thunderstorm
tolbooth	old courthouse/jail
we'an	child
wee	small
wynd	lane

LAUNDRY AND DRY CLEANING

Most finer hotels will take care of your laundry and dry cleaning needs (for a steep price, of course). But there are several establishments in the city center to cater to the politicians, business people, and bankers working in the surrounding area. Johnson's Cleaners (23 Frederick Street, New Town; Tel. 225 8095) offers express and standard service.

M

MAPS

A selection of Edinburgh maps can be found in tourist information centers. These will be adequate for sightseeing, particularly on foot. If you intend to travel by car, a more detailed map will be needed. The A–Z Map Company produces detailed maps of all cities in the UK; these can be bought at major newsagents, bookshops, and large fuel stations.

MEDIA

The main Scottish national newspaper is the *Scotsman.* Major British daily broadsheet newspapers available around the nation include the *Times,* the *Telegraph,* and the *Guardian,* which all cover world events. Daily tabloid newspapers include the *Sun* and the *Daily Mirror.* A number of newsagents in the city center sell foreign newspapers, including American titles (US papers might be one day old).

Five television networks operate in Britain: BBC1, BBC2, ITV, Channel 4, and Channel 5. Scotland produces its own BBC programs of a topical nature. Some hotels will provide satellite services such as Sky (a British network) and CNN. Check before making a booking if this is a service you require. The BBC provides national and local radio services.

A particularly useful entertainment magazine is *The List,* published biweekly and covering music, theater, cinema, arts, and sports in both Edinburgh and Glasgow.

MONEY

The official currency of Britain is the pound sterling (£); the pound is divided into 100 pence.

Edinburgh

Scotland produces its own notes and coins (different in design from those produced in England) that are legal tender throughout the UK. Likewise, notes and coins from England may certainly be used in Scotland.

Notes are printed in denominations of £5, £10, £20, £50, and £100. Coins are found in denominations of 1p, 2p, 5p, 10p, 20p, 50p, £1, £2, and £5.

Banks and building societies are open Monday–Friday 9am–5pm for foreign exchange. There are foreign exchange offices in the Marks and Spencer department store and at the American Express office (both of which are on Princes Street), as well as at Waverley Station and at the Edinburgh and Lothians Tourist Information Bureau.

Most banks and building societies will have ATMs that accept international debit cards: look for the Cirrus or Plus emblem on the machine. Most machines will also dispense cash advances on major credit cards.

Credit cards are widely accepted for payment in hotels, restaurants, and shops.

OPENING HOURS

Banks are open Monday–Friday 9:30am–3:30pm, though some offer extended hours in the evenings and on Saturday mornings. Business offices are generally open Monday–Friday 9am–5pm. Post offices are open Monday–Friday 9am–5:30pm and Saturday 9am–12:30pm.

Shops are usually open Monday–Saturday 9am–6:30pm and Sunday 10am–4pm. Hours may be extended during the summer.

Restaurants typically open noon–2pm and 6pm–10pm, but these hours will differ with the seasons, especially during the Festival. Pubs and taverns open 11am–11pm; those that sell food will usually serve noon–2pm and 7pm–9pm, but some will serve food all day without a break.

P

POLICE

The British police have a worldwide reputation for friendliness and the ability to give courteous directions. Police uniforms are navy blue, and you will see foot patrols (unarmed) operating regular routes in the city. Patrol cars have "POLICE" in large, black letters on the sides of the vehicles.

If you need the police, find a telephone box and dial 999. You will be connected to an operator who will put you in touch with the emergency service you require.

The headquarters of the Lothian and Borders Police is on Fettes Avenue (general inquiries: Tel. 311 3131).

POST OFFICES

Post offices can be recognized by red signs with yellow lettering. The main post office in Edinburgh is in the St. James Centre shopping mall on Leith Street, just east of Princes Street. It offers mailing services, currency exchange, and cash transfer, and it sells items such as stamps, postcards, and phone cards. Many postcard shops and newsagents will also sell stamps. In outlying areas, smaller post offices also act as small stores but will not have currency exchange or cash transfer services.

Postage: within the UK 26p; to Ireland 26p; and 43p to the US, Canada, South Africa, Australia, and New Zealand.

PUBLIC TRANSPORTATION

Buses. Edinburgh has a bus system that travels to all parts of the city as well as out to the coast and the surrounding countryside. The routes are split between several private companies, the main ones being Lothians Regional Transport and First Edinburgh. The average prices for a ride is 70p for adults and 50p for children. You can pay per trip on the bus (some companies require exact change) or buy a day ticket (currently £2.50 per adult), although the ticket is not transferable between companies.

Edinburgh

Bus services run from early morning until late into the evening, with several night buses operating on main routes into and out of the city. The main bus station is on St. Andrews Square. All public transport timetables are available at 2 Cockburn Street, Edinburgh (Tel. toll-free in the UK 0800 232323). Here you can also get details of transportation options for people with special needs.

City tour buses run from 9am to 6pm every 15 minutes in summer (every 25 minutes in winter) on a route that takes in most of the major attractions in the city. A day ticket costs £8; you can hop on and off the buses for a single daily fare as you visit the city's sights.

Taxis. Black taxis (like those in London) run all around the city. You can hail them on the street or pick them up at ranks (at Waverley Station and at the west end of East Street).

Trains. Edinburgh's Waverley Station is a major rail hub, providing service to all parts of the UK. Numerous local services are ideal for tourists who want to visit other Scottish towns such as North Berwick, Dunbar, Linlithgow, Stirling, St. Andrews, Perth, and Glasgow.

R

RELIGION

The Church of Scotland, which is Presbyterian, is the leading religious denomination in Edinburgh, along with Episcopalian, Methodist, and Roman Catholic congregations. The city also has a mosque, a synagogue, and an Eastern Orthodox church. Details of religious services are available (Tel. 557 1700).

T

TELEPHONE

The country code for the United Kingdom is **44**. When dialing from outside the UK, the city code for Edinburgh is **131**; if you are phoning Edinburgh from within the UK, dial **0131**.

Phonecalls can be make from call boxes and kiosks using coins, credit cards, and calling cards. Some older boxes might accept coins only. Phonecards of various denominations can be purchased from newsagents, post offices, and tourist information offices.

Calls can also usually be made direct from hotel rooms, but do check call charges in advance, as these are often much higher then normal direct-call tariffs. It is usually cheaper to phone from a public phone using a card.

TICKETS

Tickets for the Edinburgh International Festival are available from festival offices at The Hub, Edinburgh EH1 2NE (general inquiries Tel. 473 2001; box office Tel. 473 2000; e-mail: <boxofficeeif.co.uk>; website: <www.eif.co.uk>).

For Fringe performances contact the Fringe box office, which can be found at 180 High Street (a little below St. Giles Cathedral), Edinburgh EH1 1QS (Tel. 226 5257; website: <www.edfringe.com>).

Military Tattoo tickets can be purchased from the Military Tattoo office at 32 Market Street, Edinburgh EH1 1QB (Tel. 225 1188; fax 225 8627; website: <www.edintattoo.co.uk>). You can make telephone bookings from January each year or buy tickets in person starting in July. This office will also make reservations for the *Royal Yacht Britannia* in Leith.

There is no official central booking agency for theatre performances during other times of the year. The Edinburgh and Lothians Tourist Board, however, will be able to give contact details for each individual venue.

TIME ZONES

The UK runs on Greenwich Mean Time (GMT) in winter and on British Summer Time (BST) in summer. The clocks are put forward one hour on the last Saturday in March, and put back again on the last Saturday in October. The following chart shows the times in various cities during the summer:

Edinburgh

San Francisco	New York	**Edinburgh**	Sydney	Auckland
4am	7am	**noon**	9pm	11pm

TIPPING

Hotels and restaurants often add a service charge (10% to 15%) to the bill, in which case there is no need to tip. If service has not been satisfactory, this charge may be deducted from the bill. If the charge has not been added to the bill, 10% to 15% is an average tip for satisfactory service.

Taxi drivers and hairdressers do not include service charges; a tip of 10% to 15% is normal for satisfactory service.

TOILETS

There are public facilities in department stores along Princes Street; at the western end of Princes Street Gardens; and Waverley Station (also with showers). There might be a small charge for the use of some facilities. Most tourist attractions will also have public toilet facilities.

TOURIST INFORMATION

The main information center for the Edinburgh and Lothians Tourist Board (called the "Edinburgh and Scotland Information Centre" because it supplies information about all areas of Scotland) is at 3 Princes Street (Tel. 473 3800). It is open seven days a week all year (Oct–April 9am–6pm; May, Jun, and Sept 9am–7pm; Jul–Aug 9am–8pm). There is also a branch at Edinburgh International Airport, open daily all year (Nov–Mar 9am–6pm; Apr–Oct 8:30am–9:30pm). For general information, visit the website at <www.edinburgh.org>.

If you require additional information about Edinburgh (or any other area in the UK) before you travel, you can also contact the British Tourist Authority, with offices around the world (website: <www.visitbritain.com>).

In the UK: British Visitors Centre, 1 Regent Street, Piccadilly Circus, London SW1Y 4ST; Tel. 0171 808 3800 (Mon–Fri 9am–6:30pm, Sat–Sun 10am–4pm).

Australia: Level 16 Gateway, 1 Macquarie Place, Sydney NSW 2000; Tel. (2) 9377 4400; fax (2) 9377 4499.

Canada: Suite 120, 5915 Airport Road, Mississuaga, Ontario L4V 1T1; Tel. (905) 405 1720; fax (905) 405 8490.

Ireland: 18/20 College Green, Dublin 2; Tel. (1) 670 8100; fax (1) 670 8244.

New Zealand: 3rd floor, Dilworth Building (corner Queen and Customs Streets), Auckland 1; Tel. (9) 303 1446; fax (9) 377 6965.

South Africa: Lancaster Gate, 2196 Hyde Park Lane, Johannesburg; Tel. (011) 325 0343; fax (011) 325 0344

US: *Miami:* 1 Columbus Center, Alhambra Plaza, Suite 1465, Coral Gables FL 33134; Tel. (305) 529 9444; fax (305) 529 1812 (not open to the public).

New York City: 551 Fifth Avenue, Suite 701, New York NY 10176-0799; Tel. toll-free in the US (800) GO 2 BRITAIN, (212) 986 2266; fax (212) 986 1188.

Los Angeles: 10880 Wilshire Blvd., Suite 570, Los Angeles CA 90024; Tel. (310) 470 2782; fax (310) 470 8537.

W

WEBSITES

Here are a few sites to help you plan your trip on the Internet. Others can be found in the contact details for individual attractions, hotels, and restaurants in this pocket guide.

Edinburgh and Lothians Tourist Board: <www.edinburgh.org>

Edinburgh's summer festivals: <www.edinburghfestivals.co.uk>

British Tourist Authority: <www.visitbritain.com>

Railway travel and ticketing: <www.raileurope.com>

British Airways: <www.british-airways.com>

Edinburgh

American Airlines: <www.aa.com>

Qantas Airways: <www.qantas.com>

South African Airways: <www.saa.co.sa>

WEIGHTS AND MEASURES

Britain operates (at least officially) on the metric system for weights and measures, although you will commonly see signs and measures using the traditional English/Imperial system.

Length

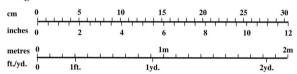

Weight

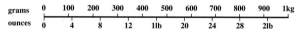

Temperature

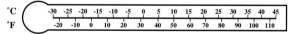

YOUTH HOSTELS

The Scottish Youth Hostels Association central booking office is at 7 Glebe Crescent, Stirling, FK8 2JA (Tel. 01786 891400; fax 01786 891333; website: <www.syha.org.uk>). You can make reservations directly through the website.

The SYHA has a hostel at 18 Eglinton Crescent, Edinburgh EH12 (Tel. 337 1120).

Recommended Hotels

Edinburgh offers accommodations ranging from five-star hotels to guesthouses, bed-and-breakfast establishments, and rooms in private homes (see ACCOMODATIONS, page 108). They are typically priced per person, per night, and include breakfast in the room charge. There might be a single person supplement if only one person uses the room. Hotels will also quote a rate for dinner, bed, and breakfast (DB&B), which — if you plan to eat in the hotel — will usually be a good value.

Guesthouses often have rooms that are just as luxurious as hotel rooms, though often without private bath facilities, concierge, staffed front desk, or in-room telephones. But they are run by local families, and you will usually get a warm welcome and a huge breakfast.

High season in Edinburgh is from June to mid-September (with an extra-high season during the Edinburgh International Festival), when it is important to make a booking if you want to guarantee a certain type of room. There are many thousands of rooms in the city, but many do not have private facilities and the best accommodation will always be booked first.

If you arrive in Edinburgh without a reservation, the tourist information offices at Waverley Street Shopping Centre (next to the railway station) and at Edinburgh International Airport will have information available and will be able to make a booking for you.

To phone a hotel in this guide from outside the UK, dial the country code (44), the city code for Edinburgh (131), and the seven-digit number. From within the UK but outside the city, dial 0131 before the number.

The price categories below are average daily rates per person per room, including breakfast and private bath (unless otherwise indicated) and VAT but not other service charges.

$$$$$	over £100
$$$$	£60–£100
$$$	£40–£60
$$	£25–£40
$	under £25

Edinburgh

Ailsa Craig Hotel $$ *24 Royal Terrace EH7 5AH; Tel. 556 1022; fax 556 6055; Web site: <www.townhousehotels.co.uk.>* Situated on the northern flank of Calton Hill, a five-minute walk to Princes Street. Part of a Georgian terrace, an elegant budget hotel with simply furnished rooms. 18 rooms. Major credit cards.

Balmoral Hotel $$$$ *1 Princes Street EH2 2QE; Tel. 556 2414; fax 557 3747.* A Princes Street landmark, overlooking the Georgian streets right at the heart of shopping yet only a couple of minutes from the Royal Mile. This luxury hotel has high standards and levels of service. Indoor pool, sauna, solarium, fitness center, and two restaurants. A two-minute walk from the railway station (rooms are soundproofed). 186 rooms. Major credit cards.

The Bonham $$$$ *35 Drumsheugh Gardens EH3 7RN; Tel. 623 6060, 226 6050; fax 226 6080; Web site: <www.thebonham. com.>* Only five minutes from the west end of Princes Street, this Victorian house has been transformed into an individual hotel with contemporary designer interiors. The Bonham offers a Mediamax system in each room, allowing DVD games, videos/stereo, free Internet access. Restaurant specializes in California cuisine. 48 rooms. Major credit cards.

Bruntsfield Hotel $$ *69–74 Bruntsfield Place EH10 4HH; Tel. 229 1393; fax 229 5634; e-mail: <bruntsfield@queensferry-hotels.co.uk>.* Overlooking the parkland of Bruntsfield Links, yet only 2-km (1.2-miles) from the city center, with shops and restaurants within strolling distance and a major bus route to town outside the door. Restaurant and bar. 75 rooms (prices are per room). Major credit cards.

The Caledonian Hotel $$$$$ *Princes Street EH1 2AB; Tel. 459 9988; fax 225 6632.* The Grand Dame of the city for many years, this hotel was originally built to form part of the terminus of the Caledonian Railway, which has now disappeared. Within a few minutes' walk of all major attractions, shops, and theaters. Full fitness complex. 249 rooms. Major credit cards.

Channings $$$$ *15 South Learmonth Gardens EH4 1EZ; Tel. 315 2226; fax 332 9631; Web site: <www.channings.co.uk>.* Five Edwardian townhouses have been transformed into a hotel retaining its original features but with comfortable, individually styled accommodations. A 10-minute walk from Princes Street. Bar/brasserie with modern conservatory dining area at rear. 48 rooms. Major credit cards.

Classic Guest House $–$$ *50 Mayfield Road EH9 2NH; Tel. 667 5647; fax 662 1016; e-mail: <info@classichouse.demon.co.uk>.* Formerly an elegant Victorian house, situated near bus route to city (five minutes into town) or 20-minutes on foot. Extremely good value for money. All rooms no-smoking, with TV, tea- and coffee-making facilities, hair dryer, and iron. 7 rooms. Major credit cards.

Dalhousie Castle $$$–$$$$$ *Bonnyrigg Midlothian EH19 3JB; Tel. (01875) 820153; fax (01875) 821936; e-mail: <enquiries@dalhousiecastle.co.uk>.* A 13th-century castle, with some rooms located in a nearby lodge (always specify castle rooms when making a booking if that is your preference). Seven miles from Edinburgh city center. Fitness center and restaurant; Scottish Nights entertainment in summer. 34 rooms. Major credit cards.

Dean Hotel $–$$ *10 Clarendon Crescent EH4 1PT; Tel. 332 0308; fax 315 4089; e-mail: <deanhotel@aol.com>.* This small, cozy, family-run hotel (a five-minute walk from the west end of Princes Street) provides a friendly welcome. 9 rooms (only 5 with private bath). Major credit cards.

Edinburgh Crowne Plaza $$$$ *80 High Street, Royal Mile EH1 1TH; Tel. 557 9797; fax 557 9789.* On the Royal Mile, this hotel has everything on its doorstep. With its exterior the tall façade of a traditional Edinburgh tenement, the luxury rooms inside are modern. Facilities include leisure club and swimming pool. 238 rooms. Major credit cards.

Frederick House Hotel $$ *42 Frederick Street EH2 1EX; Tel. 226 1999; fax 624 7064.* This new hotel has been converted from a chamber office building and offers comfortable accommodations in the central New Town. Complimentary breakfast is served at a nearby café. Satellite TV. 43 rooms. Major credit cards.

George Intercontinental Hotel $$$$–$$$$$ *19–21 George Street EH2 2PB; Tel. 225 1251; fax 226 5644; e-mail: <edinburgh@interconti.com>.* This large hotel is situated on one of the main streets of the New Town, its Georgian façade housing a luxury interior with a grand, marble foyer. Satellite TV; restaurant. Limited parking. 195 rooms. Major credit cards.

Grange Hotel $$$$ *8 Whitehouse Terrace EH9 2EU; Tel. 667 5681; fax 668 3300; Web site: <www.grange-hotel-edinburgh.co.uk>.* A large, Gothic mansion now converted into a country house hotel, the Grange offers quiet accommodations amid spacious grounds, yet it's only 3-km (nearly 2-miles) from the city center. Rooms vary in size, so make inquires when booking. Ample free parking; restaurant. 15 rooms. Major credit cards.

Greens Hotel $$$ *24 Eglinton Crescent EH12 5BY; Tel. 337 1565; fax 346 2990; Web site: <www.british-trust-hotels.co.uk>.* Recently upgraded hotel on a New Town crescent, with renovated rooms. Satellite TV; 24-hour room service. 55 rooms. Major credit cards.

Howard Hotel $$$$$ *34 Great King Street EH3 6QH; Tel. 557 3500; fax 557 6515; Web site: <www.thehoward.com>.*

The Howard — three Georgian townhouses dating from 1829 — is a luxurious and intimate hotel offering the best in hospitality. Individually designed rooms with sumptuous appointments and décor. Small lounge, room service, small car park, and the 36 Restaurant on the ground floor. 15 rooms. Major credit cards.

Jarvis Ellersly Country House Hotel $$$$ *Ellersly Road EH 12 6HZ; Tel. 337 6888; fax 313 2543.* An Edwardian country house with a wealth of period features set in expansive gardens, yet only 3 km (two miles) from the city center. Murrayfield rugby stadium nearby. Satellite TV; restaurant, room service, ample parking. 57 Rooms. Major credit cards.

Jurys Edinburgh Inn $$–$$$ *43 Jeffrey Street EH1 1DG; Tel. 200 3300; fax 200 0400; e-mail: <neil_lane@jurys.com>.* This large, modern hotel is centrally located near Waverley Station. Rooms are comfortable, with good value for the price. Satellite TV; restaurant. 186 rooms. Major credit cards.

Lauderville Guest House $$ *52 Mayfield Road EH9 2NH; Tel. 667 7788; fax 667 2636; e-mail: <lauderville_guest_house@ cableinet.co.uk>.* A registered Victorian terrace house located 6 km (4 miles) south of the city, close to main bus routes. All rooms are non-smoking and equipped with coffee-making facilities, TV, and iron. First-floor rooms available. Lounge and gardens, parking. 10 rooms. Major credit cards.

Lodge Hotel $$ *6 Hampton Terrace EH12 5JD; Tel. 337 3682; fax 313 1700; e-mail: <the lodgehotel@btconnect.com>.* This elegant Victorian house — now a small, family-run hotel — is on the road from the city to the zoo, just a 15-minute stroll to Edinburgh's center. It has car parking and a bar. 10 rooms. Major credit cards.

Edinburgh

Malmaison $$$ *1 Tower Place, Leith EH6 7DB; Tel. 555 6868; fax 555 6999; Email: <edinburgh@malmaison.com>.* Award-winning with contemporary décor, this is certainly one of the best mid-range hotels in the UK. Beautifully designed rooms have a modern feel, with CD player (and range of CDs), satellite TV, and data port all standard. Fitness room. Prices are per room (not per person), breakfast not included. The hotel has an excellent brasserie. 60 rooms. Major credit cards.

Newington Guest House $$ *18 Newington Road EH9 1QS; Tel. 667 3356; fax 667 8307; Web site: <www.newington-gh.co.uk>.* Attractive, vine-covered guesthouse, family run and located on a main bus route to the city (about five minutes to the center). All 8 rooms have TV (only 5 with private bath). Major credit cards.

Point Hotel $$$ *34 Bread Street EH3 9AF; Tel. 221 5555; fax 221 9929.* Stylish yet reasonably priced, situated to the southwest of the castle in the heart of the theatre district. Ideal for sightseeing (a stroll to the major attractions) and nights on the town. Satellite TV; room service and café bar. 95 rooms. Major credit cards.

Royal Terrace Hotel $$$$–$$$$$ *18 Royal Terrace EH7 5AQ; Tel. 557 3222; fax 557 5334.* On the northern flank of Calton Hill, a five-minute walk to Princes Street. Part of a Georgian terrace, with sumptuous period décor in public areas. Elegant rooms, most with spa baths. Satellite TV; swimming pool. 108 rooms. Major credit cards.

Simpson Hotel $$ *79 Lauriston Place EH3 9HZ; Tel. 622 7979; fax 622 7900.* Housed in a neo-Gothic mansion (ca. 1879) and close to the Royal Infirmary, this hotel offers excellent budget accommodations. The newly renovated rooms have refrigerator with self-service breakfast. Ten-minute walk from the Royal Mile. No restaurant on the premises, but plenty nearby. 62 rooms. Major credit cards.

Recommended Restaurants

Edinburgh has many fine eateries, and the range of cuisine is wide enough to satisfy almost every taste. Typical Scottish ingredients such as Aberdeen Angus beef, salmon, and game take pride of place, and quality restaurants featuring local cuisine have formed an association called "A Taste of Scotland," signified by a red cup logo in advertisements. You will find additional restaurants in the Edinburgh and Lothians Tourist Board booklet "The Essential Guide to Edinburgh and Lothians."

In the summer months it is wise to make reservations for any day of the week; low-season reservations are appreciated at all times but should definitely be made at weekends. Many establishments close on Mondays.

Most restaurants offer a "table d'hôte" set price and an "à la carte" evening menu. Pubs offer a simpler choice of dishes, with specials written on chalkboards hung near the bar. For those on a budget, pubs are often the best place to find good inexpensive food. For those who enjoy fine food on a budget, choosing to eat a main meal at lunchtime will be cheaper than eating in the evening. Restaurants in Edinburgh also offer "theatre specials" for pre- or post-performance meals.

The following categories reflect the average price of a three-course meal (without drinks), per person, including VAT. Note that some listed restaurants offer a fixed meal of more than three courses. Credit cards are accepted at most restaurants, but American Express is accepted in fewer places than are MasterCard and Visa.

$$$$$	over £50
$$$$	£40–£50
$$$	£25–£40
$$	£15–£25
$	under £15

Edinburgh

36 $$$ *36 Great King Street; Tel. 556 3636.* This unique restaurant is one of the most renowned in the city. Set in the basement of the Howard Hotel (a Georgian building), it has a very modern interior. Traditional ingredients are prepared in contemporary ways. Open for lunch Monday–Saturday noon–2:30pm, Sunday noon–2pm; dinner Monday–Saturday 7pm–10pm, Sunday 7pm–9:30pm. Major credit cards.

Atrium $$$$ *10 Cambridge Street (by the Traverse Theatre); Tel. 228 8882; fax 228 8808.* Beautifully designed restaurant with excellent food and a good reputation. Situated in the business and theater district, it is very popular at lunch and dinner. Mediterranean food with some Scottish dishes. Open Monday–Saturday for lunch noon–2:30pm, dinner 6:30pm–10:30pm. Major credit cards.

Ayutthaya $-$$ *14b Nicholson Street; Tel. 556 9351.* Authentic Thai cuisine served in a picturesque restaurant just a short distance from the Festival Theatre, in the heart of the student area. Open daily for lunch noon–2:30pm, dinner 5:30pm–10pm. Major credit cards.

Bann's Vegetarian Café $-$$ *5 Hunter Square; Tel. 226 1112.* Popular restaurant serving a range of vegetarian dishes throughout the day. Mixed clientele, from Edinburgh students and locals to visitors. Open daily 10am–11pm. Major credit cards.

Blue Bar Café $$ *10 Cambridge Street; Tel. 221 1222; fax 228 8808.* Trendy café/restaurant serving simple European dishes (in same building as Atrium). A great place to meet Edinburgh's young and fashionable. Open daily for lunch noon–2:30pm, dinner 6:30pm–10:30pm. Major credit cards.

Daniel's Bistro $$-$$$ *88 Commercial Street, Leith; Tel. 553 5933.* Serving provincial French cooking, plus Scottish and other European dishes, in a pretty harbor setting. Open daily 10am–10pm. Major credit cards.

Denzler's $$$ *121 Constitution Street, Leith; Tel. 554 3268; Web site: <www.spidacom.co.uk/edg/denzlers>*. Highly rated Swiss-Scottish restaurant in the center of Leith. Owned by Swiss chef Sami Denzler, who brings his personal touch to all dishes. Open for lunch Tuesday–Friday noon–2pm, dinner Tuesday–Saturday 6:30pm–10pm. Major credit cards.

Dubh Prais $$ *123b High Street, Royal Mile; Tel. 557 5723*. This small, cellar restaurant serves the best in Scottish cuisine. Venison, hare, and salmon dishes appear regularly on the menu. Open for lunch Tuesday–Friday noon–2pm, dinner Tuesday–Saturday 6:30pm–10:30pm. Major credit cards.

Duck's at Le Marché Noir $$–$$$ *2–4 Eyre Place; Tel. 558 1608; fax 556 0798*. Duck's describes itself as a French restaurant offering modern British cooking. You get the freshest Scottish ingredients served in Continental style in cozy surroundings. Open for lunch Monday–Friday noon–2:30pm, dinner daily 6:30pm–11pm. Major credit cards.

Est Est Est $$ *135 George Street; Tel. 225 2555*. Modern, open-kitchen Italian restaurant with stainless-steel décor and bustling atmosphere: a typical trattoria with a modern twist. All the usual dishes from minestrone, bruschetta, pizza, pasta, and grilled meats to tiramisu and ice cream. Open daily noon–10:30pm. Major credit cards.

Henderson's Salad Bar $ *94 Hanover Street; Tel. 225 2131*. Edinburgh's original vegetarian/whole-food restaurant and still said to be the best. Lively cosmopolitan atmosphere — it's always busy. Organic wines. Open Monday–Saturday 8am– 10:45pm (open Sundays only during the festival).

Edinburgh

Howie's $$ *Two locations: 63 Dairy Road (Tel. 313 3334) and St. Leonard's Street (Tel. 668 2917).* Informal bistro-style restaurants with fresh tasty ingredients. French and Scottish cuisine, with lots of game and fish on a set menu that changes daily depending on the market. No alcohol license, so bring you own bottle (there is no corking fee). Open daily for lunch noon–2pm, dinner 6pm–10pm (10:30pm during the festival). Major credit cards.

Igg's $$–$$$ *15 Jeffrey Street; Tel. 557 8184.* Igg's offers the best in formal dining as well as a fine *tapas* bar open throughout the day for casual dining (located just off the Royal Mile). The restaurant is a Scottish beef club member, pledged to take meat from only quality producers. Spanish and other European dishes also. Open Monday–Saturday for lunch noon–2:30pm, dinner 6pm–10pm. Major credit cards.

Jacksons $$–$$$ *209 High Street, Royal Mile; Tel. 225 1793.* Jacksons restaurant offers a taste of Scotland, with elegant atmosphere either in the informal cellar dining room or in the more formal Georgian salon above. It's an established restaurant with a loyal clientele. Open daily for lunch noon–2:30pm, dinner 6pm–late. Major credit cards.

Keepers Restaurant $$ *13b Dundas Street; Tel. 556 5707.* With its stone floors and several small rooms, Keepers offers a rustic yet intimate dining experience for Scottish cuisine with a Continental twist. Top suppliers for all produce guarantee the freshest and highest-quality ingredients. Open for lunch Tuesday–Friday noon–2pm, dinner Tuesday–Saturday 6pm–10pm. Major credit cards.

Kweilin $$–$$$ *19-21 Dundas Street; Tel. 557 1875; fax 557 3663.* A long-established Cantonese restaurant offering freshly prepared dishes plus an extensive wine list. Open for lunch Tuesday–Sunday noon–5pm, dinner Tuesday–Saturday 5pm–11pm. Major credit cards.

Magnum $–$$ *1 Albany Street; Tel. 557 4366.* Large bar with comfortable stylish seating areas. Good-value pub food: pies, stews, and roasts along with lighter fare such as sandwiches. Selection of wines and single-malt whiskies. Pub open Monday–Saturday 11am–11pm, with lunch service noon–2:30pm, dinner 6pm–9:30pm. Major credit cards.

Martin's Restaurant $$$ *70 Rose Street, North Lane; Tel 225 3106.* In a narrow alley in the heart of the New Town, this small, cozy restaurant serves the best in Scottish food. Specialties include dishes using Scottish game birds. Open for lunch Tuesday–Friday noon–1:50pm, dinner Tuesday–Saturday 7pm–9:45pm. Major credit cards.

Number One $$$–$$$$ *1 Princes Street (at the Balmoral Hotel); Tel. 557 6727.* Number One offers the finest in classic and contemporary dining, using the best of ingredients complemented by a fine wine list. A formal restaurant that is happy to accommodate children. Open for lunch Monday–Friday noon–2pm, dinner Sunday–Thursday 7pm–10pm and Friday–Saturday 7pm–10:30pm. Major credit cards.

Pancho Villa's Restaurant $$–$$$ *240 Canongate, Royal Mile; Tel. 557 4416.* Owner Mayra Nuñez ensures a great Latin atmosphere in this informal Mexican restaurant, which is a great place to chill out after a day's sightseeing. Open Monday–Friday for lunch noon–2:30pm and dinner 6pm–10:30pm (in summer, noon–10:30pm weekdays); Saturday noon–11pm; Sunday 6pm–10pm. Major credit cards.

Edinburgh

The Shore Bar and Restaurant $$–$$$ *3 "The Shore," Leith; Tel. 553 5080.* Historic hostelry (dating from the 18th century) that prides itself on its Scottish seafood dishes prepared without elaborate garnish. Entrées change daily depending on the catch. Open for lunch Monday–Saturday noon–2:30pm and Sunday 12:30pm–3pm; dinner daily 6:30pm–10pm.

Stac Polly $$–$$$ *Two locations: 29–33 Dublin Street (Tel. 556 2231) and 8–10 Grindlay Street (Tel. 229 5405).* Stac Polly has gained a reputation throughout the city for exciting Scottish dishes using local ingredients, for which it's won a number of awards. Authentic décor adds to a real Scottish evening. Open for lunch Monday–Friday noon–2pm, for dinner daily 6pm–11pm. Major credit cards.

Tower Restaurant $$$ *At the Museum of Scotland, 18–27 Chambers Street; Tel. 225 3003.* Restaurant with a sleek, modern interior and large windows and terrace overlooking the city streets. Scottish menu with "nouvelle" twist. Open Monday–Saturday noon–11pm (theater menu available). Major credit cards.

Veranda Restaurant $–$$ *17 Dalry Road; Tel. 337 5828; Web site: <www.theveranda.co.uk>.* Established 20 years ago, this restaurant serves probably the best Indian food in Scotland and is one of the premier Indian restaurants in the UK, popular with locals and visitors alike. The chefs have won many awards. Open daily for lunch noon–2:15pm, dinner 5pm–11:45pm. Major credit cards.

Witchery by the Castle $$$ *Castlehill, Royal Mile; Tel. 225 5613.* Set just below the castle Esplanade, the two historic dining rooms are striking in their splendor and are lit only by candles at night. Scottish and European fare; award-winning wine list. Open daily for lunch noon–4pm, dinner 5:30pm–11:30pm. Major credit cards.

INDEX